SCAMPS
AND
SCOUNDRELS

True Stories of Maritime
Lives and Legends

P147

Bob Kroll

NIMBUS
PUBLISHING

Nimbus Publishing Limited
3731 Mackintosh St, Halifax, NS B3K 5A5
(902) 455-4286 nimbus.ca

Printed and bound in Canada

Author photo: Mary Reardon
Interior and cover design: Jenn Embree
NB #: 1094

Library and Archives Canada Cataloguing in Publication
    Kroll, Robert E., 1947-, author
    Scamps and scoundrels : true stories of Maritime lives
    and legends / Bob Kroll.
    Issued in print and electronic formats.
    ISBN 978-1-77108-034-7 (pbk.).—ISBN 978-1-77108-035-4 (pdf).—
    ISBN 978-1-77108-037-8 (mobi).—ISBN 978-1-77108-036-1 (epub)
1. Maritime Provinces—Biography. 2. Maritime Provinces—History—
Miscellanea. I. Title.

FC2029.K763 2013   971.5009'9   C2013-903462-5
                                      C2013-903463-3

Nimbus Publishing acknowledges the financial support for its publishing activities from the Government of Canada through the Canada Book Fund (CBF) and the Canada Council for the Arts, and from the Province of Nova Scotia through the Department of Communities, Culture and Heritage.

❦ For Karen ❦

Contents

Preface

My ancestors lived in obscurity. Yours probably did too. We will not see our family names on urban street signs or carved into signposts along country roads. We will not find the lives of our ancestors recorded in history books or televised in film documentaries. There is little lustre to most of our family names and little glamour to the daily doings of our ancestors.

With some digging into historical records, we might find our ancestors' names on military muster roles, on ships' passenger lists, or among the names drawn for house lots in the first weeks of a settlement. The names of our ancestors might be found on deeds, wills, and church registers. Some may only appear on the back pages of a family Bible or chiselled into cold stone in a cemetery. And a few of us might even discover an ancestor among the dusty files of the criminal courts.

For most of us, our ancestors were everyday men and women who preserved their names in the lives of their children and their children's children. They were common people who wrote their lives in the mud and rocks of the Maritime provinces; people who wore gristle from bone in relative obscurity and left to history not much more than a ragged scrap about their lives and the family legacy of their names.

I collected and wrote the following stories for these ordinary people. I tried to gather the ragged scraps of their lives and braid them into a narrative that reflects the everyday of the long ago. I also tried to capture the colour of the times in which they lived and the flavour of their language.

Some of the stories are tender. Some are humorous. Some are tragic. Others are brutal. Still others reflect men and women caught in the maelstrom of living. The stories are true. The people were real.

As in my previous collection of true stories of Maritime lives, *Rogues and Rascals*, the historical sources for the following are principally government documents, newspapers, court cases, coroner reports, grand jury books, police blotters, family papers, diaries, scrapbooks, local histories, and secondary sources.

It took more than thirty years to research these stories. I did not do it alone. Heidi MacDonald helped research Prince Edward Island, and B.J. Grant covered off New Brunswick.

—B. K.

Jack Sauce
and Billy
Be-Goddamned

YOU CAN'T FIGHT CITY HALL

Ben Shorer risked his life cutting firewood for the Halifax settlers and mast spars for His Majesty's government. He had a small schooner that he sailed along the Nova Scotia coast and into various coves and inlets. He and others would anchor, row ashore, and knock down a few trees, then limb them and chunk up the branches into firewood. They would cut tree trunks to length for building boards, and longer ones for mast spars. It would take the logging crew nearly a week to get a load. And that's where the part about Ben Shorer risking his life comes in.

This was in the years between 1749 and 1757, and Ben was working outside the protection of the palisade that surrounded the settlement of Halifax. He carried a musket and an old navy pistol, but they hardly afforded the protection he would need if a few Mi'kmaq warriors and a patrol of French soldiers happened by. England was still at odds with France, and the French were allies with the Mi'kmaq, and neither cared much for the English.

One would think Ben's firewood and mast spars came at a premium, due to his working away from home under circumstances that increased the chance of losing his life. But the government took a different view. It discounted Ben's services and undervalued his products. Sometimes the government paid less than Ben's asking price. At other times, it didn't pay him at all.

On March 29, 1757, Ben Shorer petitioned the Nova Scotia government for money it owed him for firewood and mast spars. Charles Lawrence was governor of the province, and when he read Ben's petition, he refused. Governor Lawrence offered no explanation. He just ordered the government paymaster not to pay. And when Ben complained, perhaps a little too loudly, the provost marshal visited Ben's lumberyard and charged him with unlawfully selling beer and spirits.

In his petition, Ben claimed the charge was bogus, a way for the government to get out of paying what it owed. He also noted that his trial before a judge, without a jury being present, was unjust. The only witness against Ben was one of his own servants, and that man had held a grudge against Ben from the first days of his indenture in Ben's household. On top of that, the judge did not give Ben's testimony any credence, and when Ben linked the charge with the government owing him money, the judge gavelled him into silence.

Ben was convicted, fined five pounds, and sentenced to a public whipping of thirty-nine lashes. The whipping was later dropped, but the fine stuck, and Ben had to sell his schooner to pay it.

There's a lesson in this story, one most of us already know—no matter how just your cause or how right you are, you can't fight city hall.

Like Ben Shorer, John Grant learned that lesson the hard way. On March 5, 1757, he complained to the Lords of Trade that Governor Lawrence was financially cheating the province. Grant cited several instances in which the governor and his cronies used government bounties for their own benefit. He explained that bureaucrats would draw up exorbitant estimates for government work and contracts. Then, without going to public tender, the governor issued those contracts to his friends.

Ten days later, Governor Lawrence got even. He ordered John Grant's house pulled down and offered the Halifax merchant no compensation. Grant fired off another petition, and this time the governor retaliated by ordering other merchants not to trade with John Grant, going so far as to encourage them to end their friendships with him. Since Halifax businessmen depended on government contracts, most complied with the governor's order. John Grant went out of business and was socially ostracized.

A freeholders' petition the following year seemed to support John Grant's complaint about Lawrence's iron-fisted rule. This petition accused Governor Lawrence of "partial, arbitrary, and illegal behaviour." The freeholders could not go into details, because the governor controlled the mail and had underlings screening letters and denying travel permits to certain individuals seeking to go abroad. The freeholders called Nova Scotia a virtual prison, because no one could leave without the governor's permission.

We hardly think of our ancestors living under such repression in Nova Scotia, but they did. It would take nearly a hundred years for reformers like Joseph Howe to initiate political and social change that would place government in the hands of the people and subject governors to the rule of law. Yet for all the social and political change over the past two hundred years, one thing still rings true: you can't fight city hall.

WEDDING DAYS

Most often, a weekly rural newspaper takes a kind-hearted, rose-coloured view of local affairs. Unless a crime has been committed, a small weekly press will not go out of its way to write bad things about its neighbours. And that makes the following account of a wedding in northern New Brunswick all the more unusual.

On October 18, 1934, the *Observer*—a little weekly newspaper then published in Hartland, New Brunswick—had this to say about a local wedding:

"Mr. Bill Henway and Miss Alice Livekin were married at noon Monday at the home of the bride's parents. Reverend M. L. Cassaway officiated.

"The groom is a popular young bum who hasn't done a lick of work since he got shipped in the middle of his junior year at college. He manages to dress well and keep a supply of spending money because his dad is a soft-hearted old fool who takes his bad cheques instead of letting him go to jail where he belongs.

"The bride is a skinny fast little idiot who has been kissed by every boy in town since she was twelve years old. She paints her face like a rainbow. She doesn't know how to sew, cook, or keep house.

"The bride wore some kind of white thing that left most of her legs sticking out at one end and her bony upper end sticking out the other.

"The young people will make their home with the bride's parents—which means they will sponge off the old man until he dies."

The newspaper's final remark about the wedding was this: "The happy couple anticipate the blessed event in about five months."

Here's another article about a wedding that jumped off the front page of a different newspaper: the *North Shore Leader*.

On June 8, 1917, Armette Morgan appeared before a Justice of the Peace at Tracy Station—a hamlet in southern Sunbury County, New Brunswick, on the rail line that links Saint John and Montreal—and charged Wesley Morgan, age forty, with bigamy. She said that her husband of nine years had recently gotten married to another woman.

Wesley appeared before the judge and told him how it had happened.

A few days ago, he and three others had been drinking steadily, and suddenly decided they should all get married. The others were Mrs. Thomas (a middle-aged widow recently acquitted of murdering her husband), Frank Morey (Mrs. Thomas's twenty-one-year-old boyfriend), and the youthful Violet Thomas (Mrs. Thomas's daughter). The four drove to Fredericton for a double wedding.

Wesley didn't see anything wrong with marrying young Violet, since he had rightfully purchased her from Mrs. Thomas for twenty-one dollars. He told the judge he had paid cash, which Mrs. Thomas used to buy finery for her own wedding to Frank Morey. Twenty-one dollars was a fair chunk of change in 1917, and Wesley figured that earned him the right to marry Violet, even though he was already married to Armette Morgan.

Wesley Morgan's second venture into marriage, which resulted in a charge of bigamy, cost him a twenty-dollar fine and two years in Dorchester Penitentiary.

The *North Shore Leader* ended the account by saying that "the people concerned have a most peculiar view on matrimony."

PURE LUCK

Against the overwhelming force of a natural disaster, some get lucky, and some don't.

The Miramichi Fire started as many forest fires do—lightning. Trees burst into flame in the woodlands at several places along the Miramichi River in the summer of 1825. The fires smouldered for much of the summer, one that was uncommonly hot and dry.

On October 1, a strong southwest wind blew up. It fanned the smouldering fires. The wind continued blowing, and by October 4, the small fires blew into a raging firestorm sweeping towards the northeast.

That the fire was coming, Miramichiers knew well, for its smoke darkened the skies, then blackened them. By October 7, its roar shook the earth, and its glare turned darkest evening into brightest day.

Only six buildings on the Miramichi survived the fire's ravages, and it even burned three ships in the Northumberland Strait. Two hundred and fifty-three people were burned to death; the casualties among animal life were incalculable. In shallower parts of the river, the waters boiled, and cooked salmon floated belly-up.

Oddly, the fire spared some spots completely. One small patch of remaining greenery was in a small hollow where an old trapper had built his shanty. At the last moment, this pitiable man saw that his only hope was to make a dash to the river. He never made it.

After the fire subsided, an exploration team found his body. All around were hills covered with blackened rampikes, but two hundred metres farther on was a woodsy hollow, its trees still standing tall and green—and in its centre, the old trapper's shanty, completely untouched by the Miramichi Fire.

The trapper wasn't lucky. But thirty-one years later, John Campbell was.

Some people called it a miracle that John Campbell was alive, but Campbell said it was just one tragedy piled on top of another.

John Campbell lived with his family on a farm fifty kilometres outside of Sydney, Cape Breton, on the post road to St. Peters. He had a wife, three children, and two maidservants, and he looked after his aged mother.

He read the Bible to his family and attended Sunday service. He thanked the Lord every day for the sun and rain, and again whenever he had a bumper crop to harvest. In short, John Campbell was no more religious than any of his neighbours. And yet, people said it was a miracle that he was spared. But John Campbell disagreed.

In the winter of 1856, there was a fierce storm full of high winds and torrents of rain. Water ran from the highlands in a thousand rivers. With the rain came a thaw, and with the thaw came an avalanche of snow propelled forward by the flood of water.

In one fell swoop, snow descended on the Campbell house. Its sheer weight brought down the roof and walls, and crushed all within.

All except John Campbell. Neighbours found him the following day, unconscious from having been thrown headlong against the fireplace. While his family was killed and buried under tons of fallen snow, John lay on the hearth with hardly a snowflake on his body.

"A miracle," his neighbours said. But John Campbell thought otherwise. He was now cursed to live a lonely life of deepest sorrow that a few could ever understand. He would visit the graves of his family every day, and wish he had shared their fate.

GEORGE BROWN

In the 1880s, a sculling race drew thousands to the Halifax waterfront to watch the world's best oarsmen rowing for glory. Sculling was like horse racing—a gambling man's sport. And it had all the attributes of a horse race: intrigue, skill, and the promise of rich rewards.

One of the best at rowing a scull to victory was a fisherman from Herring Cove, Nova Scotia. His name was George Brown. George had a reputation that reached across the Maritimes and down into the Boston States, where the gentry took sculling seriously.

In September 1873, John Biglin, a former American sculling champ, arrived in Halifax from Boston and challenged George. When George hesitated to accept, Biglin got mouthy. He criticized George's rowing style and called him nothing but a fisherman who had out-rowed other fishermen. Still, George was noncommittal.

Then a few days later, as the betting pool grew, George waltzed down to the waterfront and announced in a quiet, reticent voice that he would face Biglin on the water.

Now it was Biglin's turn to hem and haw, postponing the race for a day, and then another and another. Biglin and his supporters saw Brown as an easy mark, and sought to delay the race so more and more money could be wagered.

On race day, George arrived on the waterfront without much fanfare. Biglin had an entourage. The two men took to their sculls, the pistol fired, and before the sculls had reached the halfway mark, it became obvious to everyone—even the uninitiated observers—that George Brown had taken the American to the cleaners. He crossed the finish line two hundred feet ahead of Biglin, and turned in the fastest time on record for a five-mile race: thirty-eight minutes and fifty-five seconds.

The following year, Brown went to Boston to race the single-scull world champion, William Scharff. The purse was four thousand dollars—big money in 1874. Newspapers billed the race as a contest of Scharff's science and skill against George Brown's brute strength. One reporter wrote that Brown used an old-fashioned fisherman's stroke. Apparently, the skinny on Brown was that "he was slow to take the water," which meant he got off to a slow start. With all the newspaper hype, the betting went wild. There were betting pools in Halifax, Saint John, Boston, Pittsburgh, and New York. The amount wagered was more than $250,000.

Brown showed up at the Boston marina with a shy, "oh-my-gosh" way about him, not talking, and mechanically adjusting his oars. Scharff was a showboat, hamming it up for the thousands who had come to watch.

Sure enough, just as predicted, George Brown got off slow, falling a half-length behind Scharrf. Scharrf's supporters quickly offered side bets and odds that Scharff would win by a full length. And just as quickly, George's backers took the bets and doubled them. To the trained eye, it was obvious that George's boys seemed to know what would happen next.

As George caught his rhythm, his scull shot forward so fast that by the four-mile marker he had a three-length lead. He held that lead to the finish line, and won by six seconds.

It's a good thing he did, because George Brown, the nonchalant fisherman from Herring Cove, Nova Scotia, had bet his life savings on himself.

ST. ANDREW'S CHURCH

In 1804, the Catholic farmers at St. Andrews, Prince Edward Island, built a beautiful church for their parish. It was post-and-beam construction, and it was big. But by 1862, it was not big enough. So the grandchildren of these Catholic farmers built another one—every bit as beautiful as the first, and even bigger.

Meanwhile, in Charlottetown, the sisters of the Congregation of Notre Dame needed a larger building for their school on Pownal Street. The farmers at St. Andrews offered their old church, which still stood tall and proud. The tricky part was moving it.

Father Dan MacDonald supervised the transportation of the church down the frozen Hillsborough River. It took months to jack up the wooden edifice and get the iron runners in place. And then on March 1, 1864, every blessed Catholic farmer from the St. Andrews community, along with a few hundred horses, showed up to make the move.

No sooner had they set their shoulders for the heave-ho than they found themselves battling a blinding snowstorm. With the church on the go, there was no stopping now. Father Dan prayed and prayed, and by the grace of God, the church skidded onto the ice and sledded down the Hillsborough River.

About ten kilometres from Charlottetown, God must have blinked, or Father Dan must have run out of holy words, because here the ice chinked into a wide fissure and swung the church to starboard. Its runners skidded, and the church plunged into two feet of crusted mud.

As it is written, for all things there is a time and a purpose under heaven. Father Dan and the sisters appealed to God and the general public for help. More than five hundred men assembled along the Hillsborough River—Catholics and Protestants alike.

They forgot the religious differences that had long divided the community, and, arm in arm—with nearly two hundred horses, and with their lips all mouthing the words to the same prayer—they pulled that church from the mud and delivered it to the sisters of the Congregation of Notre Dame in Charlottetown.

"LEWY THE INDIAN"

To look out on Halifax Harbour today, with container ships and naval traffic steaming in and out, and with passenger ferries chugging steadily back and forth between Dartmouth and Halifax, one would hardly think that once upon a time, the harbour froze over.

Maybe not solid enough in the centre of the harbour to prevent ships from coming and going, but solid enough for one man to think he could run to the middle to catch an outgoing ship.

On February 4, 1815, the brig *Clinker* had raised anchor in the middle of Halifax Harbour and prepared to set sail for England. A man raced along the waterfront, waving a stack of letters and hollering for the ship to wait. He was late with family correspondence for the *Clinker* to carry abroad. Then he saw the ice-filled harbour, and the ship tenders pulled from the water and idle on the beach. It became clear to the man that there would be no rowing to the brig to deliver the letters. His shoulders sagged with regret. Among the letters was a proposal of marriage, and as most married men know, when a young man's heart decides on love, waiting to pop the question is pure agony.

That's when "Lewy the Indian" came to the rescue. Lewy was a waterfront fixture. He ran errands for ship's captains, sailors, and merchants—just about anyone who would pay him to fetch or deliver whatever needed fetching or delivering. Lewy was as thin as a nail, with a mop of thick, black hair, a broken-toothed grin, and squinty eyes that seemed to see through the illusion of life.

The *Acadian Recorder* reported about that freezing winter morning, and how Lewy stepped from the waterfront crowd and offered to deliver the letters to the brig *Clinker* for a dollar. A dollar was a lot of money in 1815, but the man with the letters was in no position to negotiate. He looked at the ice on the harbour and at the letters in his hand; he felt the stab of love in his chest, withdrew a dollar from his purse, and begged Lewy to run for it.

Lewy did just that. He knew better than to traipse with an easy tiptoe across the cracking ice. He knew reaching that ship would take speed, and speed was what he gave. He hit the ice running like a dog-chased deer, outracing the cracks spreading underfoot. And when he reached the ice sludge churned up by the rocking ship, he leapt to a rope ladder that had been thrown over the side.

After climbing aboard and delivering the letters, Lewy now had to make it back. He descended the ladder and jumped as far from the ship as he could over the ice sludge. He landed on his feet, skidded, slipped, held his balance, and bolted for the shoreline inches ahead of the ice cracks.

Those crowding the wharves cheered him on. Some even lay bets, and those who bet against Lewy reaching safety...lost.

Lewy was the talk of the town for weeks after. He was now in high demand for running errands from the waterfront. "Fleet of foots" was how the *Acadian Recorder* described him—the man who had earned a dollar by running over thin ice.

DEEP SNOW

In the winter of 1905, it snowed nonstop for four weeks. About the only travel option that winter was sleighs drawn by heavy horse and ox teams. The deep snow shut down the railways and trunk lines from Halifax to Moncton. The railway spent a great wad of money hiring every able man to clear the main line. It did little good. The snowfall layered the tracks faster than the men could shovel.

It had started snowing on the third morning of that New Year. Tiny, white flakes sticking in the evergreens promised Charles W. Roop a sweep of wonderment as he hitched his horse for a forty-kilometre sleigh from his general store in Springfield, Nova Scotia, over South Mountain and into the Annapolis Valley, to Middletown. At this time the trains were still running, and Charlie could just as easily have taken the trunk line between Lunenburg and Middleton, and cut down his travelling time by half. But Charles W. Roop was old-fashioned. He figured he could return on that coal-choking monstrosity at night, but for going, there was nothing more pleasurable than a long winter ride along a country road, with a daydream for company, feeling the slow, youthful, almost forgotten stir of anticipation in his belly.

In his shirt pocket, under the sleigh rug and a heavy wool coat, Charlie carried an invitation from Mrs. Elmira Stoddard, who was three years a widow. Mrs. Elmira had asked for an afternoon of Charlie's company. She wanted him to meet her schoolteacher sister, who lived an isolated life at Mount Hanley, on the Fundy side of North Mountain. The sister's name was Miss Emma Brown.

Charlie was sixty-eight, a widower, six times a father, and ten times a grandfather—and for the past twenty-two months and three days, he had been alone.

It snowed steadily most of that morning, which made sleighing the old Lunenburg Road over Whynot's Hill and through Nictaux Falls a smooth run. An easy wind made it comfortable for the horse steaming on the upgrades and making time along the flats. It was comfortable for Charlie too, who enjoyed the backcountry quiet of a snowfall, the way the flakes blew through the woodland and fields, and gathered where others before them had gathered—the way one group of people gathered behind another to make a settlement.

Charlie made Middleton in less than three hours. It took him another hour to stable his horse, arrange for a stable hand to return the horse and sleigh to Springfield, and plod the snowy streets to Mrs. Elmira's house on Ben Brown Road. It took him several minutes more to muster enough courage to climb the stairs and knock. His legs seemed to wobble from sitting so long in the sleigh—at least that's why Charlie thought they did—and his back tingled like it did when his plough struck a large rock buried in a field. Even his knock was hesitant. Mrs. Elmira commented on it, saying something about how she had expected a big, bullish pounding on the front door, but all she heard was a soft tapping.

Charlie removed his coat and checked hat. It felt almost as if his horsy ears unfolded and his grey hair spiked out like a frightened porcupine. His hands were sweaty and his mouth was dry, and his voice went raspy when Mrs. Elmira introduced him to her sister.

Emma Brown was a wisp of a woman, with tightly styled grey hair and a little smile that brightened her round face like a candle in a room full of mirrors. She was pretty at fifty-seven and would have been quite a catch when she was younger, if teaching school hadn't gotten in the way of living, and living hadn't gotten in the way of loving, and loving hadn't curled up like a winter rose left in a hot kitchen.

It was clear enough that Mrs. Elmira was matchmaking a husband for Miss Emma, and that Charlie was not the first—nor would he be the last—to come for an afternoon's visit so she and Emma could test out the pleasure of his company. Charlie didn't mind, though. A woman had as much reason as a man to size up the stock before an auction. Besides, a three-hour sleigh on a country road through snow-blown woods and frozen fields, followed by two hours in the company of two gracious women, was satisfaction enough without wishing himself the blue ribbon from Miss Emma Brown. And yet, he did.

Maybe that's why he felt so uncomfortable in Elmira Stoddard's front parlour, with a teacup too dainty for his hand, and his tongue rolling around the inside of his mouth. He fed the fire to break the silences, which were long and often.

At four o'clock, Charlie said he should leave soon to catch the 6:15 train to Springfield, and received no objection from Mrs. Elmira—not until he opened the front door, and all three saw how the wind was blowing a blizzard across the town. "No train running in this," said Mrs. Elmira, like she knew for certain. Miss Emma insisted that Charlie stay with them until the storm blew out. She felt obligated, she said, because it was their invitation that had brought Charlie to Middleton in the first place. Besides, no God-fearing Christian would send another human being into such a blow. Mrs. Elmira agreed, and was already fixing Charlie the daybed in the kitchen.

During supper that night, the sisters talked about how a fierce winter storm always played rough with the world, like a kitten with a ball of yarn, and how, also like a kitten, a storm soon settled down to a soft purr. Each promised the other, and Charlie too, that tomorrow would be as quiet and untroubled as a sleeping cat.

After supper, Charlie lugged in logs from the woodshed and stacked them beside the wood stove in the parlour, behind the cookstove in the kitchen, and alongside the cylinder stove on the upstairs landing. He had a smoke in the woodshed and felt better for it. Then he joined the sisters in the parlour. Each was squinting over needlepoint beside lamps that smoked from having their wicks turned up a little too high. Charlie watched the shadows of the sisters' hands dancing on the wall, and the way the lamplight honeyed Miss Emma's cheeks and combed strands of gold into her grey hair. He listened to the storm, and several times checked its progress from the window.

Maybe it was the look of that storm piling snow on the road, and the fierce wind drifting it against the houses and barns, rattling the windows, and coughing smoke back down the chimney. Or maybe it was the comfort of the parlour light, and the way Miss Emma smiled at him for the way he dropped his eyes when she caught him looking. Or maybe it was the splay of his shadow on the wall in the company of others. Whatever it was, something brought a song into Charlie's mind: a ballad. He sang it. Soft at first, then deepening on the chorus, the way it was meant to be sung.

After the first verse, Miss Emma had picked up the melody, and by the time Charlie hit the chorus for the second time, she was at the upright piano in the corner, playing with both hands to Charlie's song. Mrs. Elmira hummed along, and together they gave the next verse a sadness that would have squeezed tears from a stump.

Charlie held the last note for the longest time, as though unwilling to let go of this bond he felt with Miss Emma. Then his voice cracked and they all laughed, and as the laughter trailed, Miss Emma played the opening bar to "If I were a Blackbird," knowing Charlie and Mrs. Elmira would know the words.

The following evening, they sang hymns. The singing seemed to plough Charlie's mouth of stones and sow his mind with a whole lot of things to say. When the three were not singing, they were taking turns talking. Miss Emma talked about teaching school in Mount Hanley, and Charlie about storekeeping in Springfield. They talked about growing up and growing old, and about the everyday of living. By the time they looked up from all this singing and talking, a week had come and gone, and still it snowed.

By day, Miss Emma read and prepared her lessons for when school started up again. Mrs. Elmira fussed, cooked, and cleaned. And Charlie fixed what had not been fixed since Mrs. Elmira's husband had died.

Another day passed in the same way, then another.

It took a further two days to clear the tracks to Springfield. On the tenth day, Charlie said goodbye to Miss Emma Brown and Mrs. Elmira Stoddard at the railway station and headed for home.

Charlie was a simple man, who used simple words to express the cold shiver he felt upon returning to his empty house. There was no contrivance in what Charlie wrote. No practiced expression. No glossy way of saying it. He sat at the fire for three nights before taking pen to paper and writing to Miss Emma that he preferred talk to silence, and the pleasure of her company to the loneliness of shadows. He asked her to marry him, and signed his name— Charles W. Roop.

Miss Emma took forty-eight hours to answer. She too knew the economy of words. She wrote that she would be pleased to marry him, and signed her name—Miss Emma Brown.

They married on July 17, 1905. They practically sang their vows to each other. They kept on singing together most evenings after that—sometimes off-key, but so what?

On June 14, 1923, Charlie's heart gave out while he was turning sod in the garden. He was eighty-five. Emma buried him on a hill overlooking a lake in the family graveyard, the whole of which was framed by the kitchen window where Emma sat most days, warming herself by the cookstove and taking tea. In winter, she watched the snow piling on Charlie's grave and smiled to remember his visit to Middletown at the time of the Deep Snow of 1905. It was the deepest snow there ever was, she thought, but deep snow was nothing compared to the deep love she felt for that shy, horse-eared man who had sung his way into her heart.

THE PEI TUNNEL

The concrete-and-steel bridge over the Northumberland Strait between New Brunswick and Prince Edward Island is new—but the whole idea of a tunnel under the strait, that's about a hundred years old.

Part of PEI's deal when it joined Confederation was "continuous communication" with the mainland. Islanders knew the easy back and forth flow of goods, services, and information put money in their pockets.

In summer, there were no complaints. The Northumberland Strait was crowded with ship traffic. But in winter, iceboats and icebreakers were slow and not always dependable. In 1885, George Howlan of the *Charlottetown Examiner* raised the banner for a submarine tunnel between the mainland and Prince Edward Island, and the idea caught fire. Islanders could hardly think or talk about anything else. The clergy preached the submarine tunnel from their pulpits, politicians promised it, and engineers swore it was possible. After all, the British had already tunnelled under the Thames River, so why not the Northumberland Strait?

Engineers made surveys and studies, and estimated the cost at five million dollars. During the election of 1887, even John A. Macdonald got into the act, promising a submarine tunnel to Islanders. But when PEI failed to vote Conservative that year, old John A. let the idea fade into memory—at least until the next election.

That's when talk of a tunnel started all over again, during the federal election of 1891. There were more surveys and studies, and political promises made in church halls and from backs of horse-drawn wagons; then after the election, politicians let the idea peter out. Sound familiar?

ELIZABETH REGAN

Elizabeth Regan grew up on King Street in Saint John, New Brunswick, during the late 1700s. She was the daughter of a Loyalist. Her father, Jeremiah Regan, was a preacher—well educated and well cultured. It was said that he wrote his Sunday sermons in Greek and translated them into English while standing on the pulpit. And it was said that Elizabeth Regan was every bit as smart.

In 1790, Elizabeth married James Fairchild of Sussex. The road they strolled when courting is still called Regan's Road, and the place where James dropped to his knee and popped the question is still called Fairchild's Gate.

They had four girls, each one as smart as paint. Then James died when Elizabeth was only thirty-four years old. He left her with plenty of money, and Elizabeth could have stayed home in retirement. But she didn't. Instead, Elizabeth Regan Fairchild opened a school for boys in Saint John.

She started classes early, before sun-up, and worked her pupils late into the evening. She believed the best education came with hard work. Her efforts had a remarkable influence on New Brunswick life and letters during the next century.

On the day of her funeral in 1849, most Saint John businesses and government offices closed up shop so that her former pupils— many of them judges, lawyers, clergy, and businessmen—could walk in the long procession that followed her coffin to the cemetery.

YANKEE GALE

It seemed as though the entire New England fishing fleet was in the Gulf of St. Lawrence during the fall of 1851—nearly one hundred fishing boats. Most of them were sixty to one hundred tons, with ten to fourteen hands on board.

One sailor said: "On Friday night, October 3rd, the sea had a strange glassy look as though covered in oil. And it was warm. Too warm for that time of year."

That night, the wind picked up from the northeast. There was a fine rain. As the night wore on, the wind and rain increased. By noon the next day, the wind was a formidable blow. And it kept blowing for more than twenty-four hours. Old sailors said it was the strongest wind they had ever experienced.

A few New England ships were lucky enough to round the North Cape to safety. But most ran square to the wind, which tossed them on the water and dashed them on shore. The howling night filled with the sounds of shattering wood and dying men. At Rustico, Prince Edward Island, three ships wrecked on the shore within a kilometre of each other. Huge waves lifted other ships out of the water and threw them onto beaches and into meadows.

People called it the "Yankee Gale," because seventy-four New England ships were lost, and fifty were shattered beyond recognition.

In all, 160 men drowned. Rows of cadavers lined the PEI beaches like cordwood. One sailor said it was the greatest destruction by storm he had ever seen. And another agreed: "That Yankee Gale— that was a fierce blow. Worst of 'em all."

THE CAPES ROUTE

In the winter of 1827, Donald McInnis and Neil Campbell proved what most Prince Edward Islanders had long suspected: the Capes Route across the Northumberland Strait, between Cape Traverse,

PEI, and Cape Tormentine, New Brunswick, was the safest and fastest route in winter. After McInnis and Campbell's successful crossing in record time, this route became the regular winter crossing for both passengers and the Royal Mail.

Iceboats were sturdy wooden boats, sheathed with tin to withstand the grinding action of the ice. They had long iron runners. Each boat came equipped with a leather harness that fit over a man's shoulders and a leather bellyband for around the waist.

The iceboats had to be hauled over large mounds of ice, called pressure hummocks, and over long ridges of rafter ice. This could take hours. The waistband saved a man from drowning when the ice gave way or an ice cake tipped.

For passengers making a winter crossing, comfort came second to staying alive. Passengers paid five dollars to cross the Northumberland Strait in winter—two dollars if they helped the boatmen haul the boat across.

On February 20, 1847, Phillip Irving commanded an iceboat across the strait. Winter squalls are frequent on the strait, and one blew up during Irving's crossing. He and his crew had to flip the boat over for shelter, and start a fire to keep them warm in the night. They drifted twenty-five kilometres eastward on the ice flow and had to make back that distance the following day.

Three crewmen and several passengers had frostbite, including those passengers who had paid the extra three bucks for comfort.

NEW BRUNSWICK BASEBALL

Baseball's popularity caught on in the Maritimes about the same time it did in the United States: in the 1860s, during the American Civil War and during our own political struggle to tie a handful of provinces into a confederation. Maybe baseball was just what Americans and Canadians needed at that time to take their minds off war and politics.

These first games were usually part of a Sunday afternoon pastime, which in those early years violated the Lord's Day Act. In Halifax, Moncton, Saint John, and Fredericton, there was usually a brawl on Sunday between police and baseball players. The fine was five dollars, plus court costs. The law soon changed when the police and fire departments started playing too. Soon the game became something more than a pastime.

In 1871, with the US and Canada in political turmoil, baseball became a welcome relief for both countries and a source of national pride. In that year, Americans in Calais, Maine, and New Brunswickers in St. Stephen scouted each other across the St. Croix River.

There was the usual brag and bluster from both sides. Then a challenge was made. On July 9, 1871, the Frontier Club from Calais played the St. Stephen Wide Awakes (a name that was sure to send terror into their opponents' hearts) in what was probably the first World Series of Baseball. The Frontier Club mauled the St. Stepheners fifty-five to thirty-three.

"Best of three," yelled someone from the St. Stephen team. A few days later, the Calais team came back. This time it was Frontier eighty, Wide Awakes sixty-three.

It was on that day, with our country's pride on the line, that those nine St. Stepheners decided for the rest of Canada that baseball was not our national game—hockey was!

LARRY'S RIVER

In 1755, British soldiers marched through the Annapolis Valley, rounded up the Acadian settlers, and expelled them from Nova Scotia. Some Acadian families hid from the soldiers, and afterwards escaped to more unsettled regions of the province—many along the Eastern Shore, and some at the mouth of a small river that empties into Tor Bay.

After the British captured Fortress Louisburg, the French in nearby towns abandoned their homes and farms and fled for their lives. They sought refuge in the forests, where they wandered for days, until some of them came upon the Acadian settlement at the mouth of that small river.

Among the names of the first Acadian settlers there were those of Pellerine, Pettipas, Manette, Avery, and Fougere. They farmed the rocky soil and fished the bountiful sea. They built new homes for their families far enough from the coast to be hidden from English patrol boats.

For more than two centuries, Larry's River has been known as the place where the French dwell. And yet, oddly enough, none of the first French settlers gave their names to this small village. Not even Father Forrest, the Cape Breton Catholic priest who helped bring prosperity to this French settlement, was so honoured.

Instead, Larry's River is named after an Irishman, Larry Keating, whose single accomplishment and greatest historical significance is that he spent a winter in the area hunting moose.

HALFWAY HOUSE

Charles Brown obtained a land grand of two hundred acres in Athol, Cumberland County, Nova Scotia, and one day in 1814, he took to building a house on the property. He built it big, and he built it to last. He fired brick for the chimneys from clay that he dug from a nearby field.

Brown's house had nine fireplaces. The two in the cellar were arched, and large enough to stand in. There were six rooms downstairs and six up, with Christian panel doors and large window recesses. One of the downstairs rooms was a barroom with a secret door to the cellar, where Charles Brown kept his supply of rum and beer.

What Charles Brown had built was a coach house for overnight guests. He had calculated that his property lay halfway between Amherst and Parrsboro. With the two towns growing like well-fed children, there would be a lot of back and forth travel between the two, and travellers would need a place to stop over halfway along their journey. He called the building "Halfway House."

The first coach service was an ox wagon that took most of two days to bump and rumble the 125 kilometres. That was in summer. In winter, the ox wagon took nearly a week.

By 1830, a stagecoach with six horses was regularly running between the towns, making the trip a lot faster—but not fast enough to pass up dinner and a night's lodging at the Halfway House.

Charles Brown made a fortune, and when he died, Fred Baker, who owned the stagecoach business, bought the house and surrounding land and carried on with overnight stops.

All that came to an end in the 1870s with the advent of the "iron horse"—the railway. Modern times were upon us. People now took a notion to get from one place to another faster, and no longer cherished an overnight stay at the Halfway House.

A WILL TO LIVE

Auguste Le Bourdais was a mountain of a man, with hands the size of cured hams and muscles as hard as oak. He captained a three-mast schooner between the Maritimes, Quebec, and Europe.

In December 1880, Bourdais sailed to Belgium with a load of lumber. Not far from the Magdalen Islands, a screaming blizzard blew down from the Labrador coast. The wind howled like a host of banshees and tossed the ship around like a bottle. All at once, there was a loud crack of timber as the ship ran a sandbar off Coffin Island. Within minutes, the raging sea had pounded that ship into a splintered wreck.

It was nearly a week before the blizzard blew itself out. Afterwards, two Coffin Island men went out to scavenge the beach for valuables from the wreck. Suddenly, an enormous shape reared up out of the snow. The two scavengers thought it a ghost and ran for a priest.

It was Auguste Le Bourdais, wearing a twelve-inch-thick coat of ice and crusted snow. He had clung to the wreckage for two days before he washed ashore. He had to eat snow to stay alive. And by the time he was found, his legs had frozen solid and had to come off.

It took eight men to hold him down. No doctor. No chloroform. Just rough-and-ready surgery with a carpenter's saw and a sharp knife. Still, he lived another fifty-seven years, fathered a brood of children, and was considered the strongest man on the Magdalen Islands—legs or no legs. He also founded the telegraph service on the Islands and managed it until his death in 1937.

Auguste Le Bourdais was truly a man with a will to live.

ICHABOD CORBITT

Ichabod Corbitt had a lame leg, and the word around Annapolis Royal, Nova Scotia, was that because Ichabod "couldn't do, he taught." If that was the case, then Ichabod Corbitt made the most of his disability, for he taught throughout most of the last half of the nineteenth century. He started teaching at fourteen years old, and continued teaching for the next sixty years.

He lived with his wife and ten kids at the foot of St. Anthony Street in Annapolis Royal. The family occupied the downstairs, and the large room on the second floor was Ichabod's schoolroom. It held half a dozen rows of crudely made desks (of Ichabod's own construction), with deal planks for benches. The planks were held in place by used fence posts a farmer had hauled from the ground and meant to throw away.

Much of what Ichabod owned was second-hand. He was not known for his carelessness with a dollar, or for his generosity with heat. The four-foot by two-foot cast iron box stove in the classroom hardly smouldered on the coldest days. It was said that the snow his pupils tracked into the hall in winter was still there come spring.

Pupils provided their own books: a New Testament, *Goldsmith's History of England*, *Lindley Murray's Grammar*, and *Dillsworth's Spelling Book*. Recess was rare, holidays more so. The only holiday Ichabod Corbitt recognized was St. Patrick's Day, which just happened to be his birthday.

School started at nine o'clock sharp, with Corbitt roaring, "Toes out, chins in, breast full, heels together, and eyes on the master." That had the pupils sitting bolt upright for what seemed an eternity, or at least until a designated student called out, "Sun's to the mark, sir," which meant sunlight had crept far enough into the room to reach a carved mark on the window ledge. And that meant class was dismissed.

Ichabod Corbitt did not own a watch.

GOD CALLING

We take high-speed, wireless communications for granted. We may stand in line overnight waiting to buy the latest cellphone or wireless gadget, and we may beam in amazement at what each new device can do, but we are hardly surprised when these electronic marvels fulfil even our wildest imaginings. In fact, we have almost come to expect that they will.

In years gone by, ordinary folk did not dream about long-distance, wireless communication. Their expectations for wizardry hardly exceeded the simple combustion engine, and even that was a stretch for some. So when a newfangled invention called the "telephone" hit the Maritimes, some were speechless, which hindered the promotion of this new device. Others thought it was downright devilish and should be avoided at all costs. Most, however, were intrigued that their voice could be carried over a wire from one end of town to the other.

James Hawthorn was so intrigued that in 1886, he dug into his pocket and laid out the necessary cash to establish himself as owner/manager of New Brunswick's first telephone office in Fredericton.

There was nothing fancy about Jimmy Hawthorn's operation. He simply set up the switchboard at the back of his hardware store on Queen Street, and plugged in one line whenever a call came in, then another line to the household they wanted to talk to. He worked as manager, repairman, and operator for all forty-six telephone customers.

By 1889, there were more than a hundred telephones in Fredericton, and that gave Mr. Knudson, who took over from James Hawthorne, the bright idea to broadcast a church service over the phone lines. That did not go over well with most of the Fredericton clergy, but one of them was courageous enough to give it a try: Reverend William Dobson of the Wilmot Church.

Dobson reasoned that if God-fearing men and women could hear the power of his sermon over the phone line, they'd line up at the door of his church the following Sunday for the real thing. He asked his congregation to spread the word, but they didn't spread it much beyond their own membership.

On that Sunday in 1889, Mr. Knudson patched in the lines of the hundred or so subscribers, and placed a transmitter on the pulpit in the Wilmot Church. Then Reverend Dobson raised his voice with the word of God.

As the first few phone subscribers—many not knowing what was going on—lifted their home receivers to answer the call, they heard Reverend Dobson as plain as day. But as more subscribers activated their receivers, the signal became weaker. The Reverend's voice slowly faded. Soon there was an astonishing assortment of squeaks and electrical noise mixed in with a distant voice that sounded like it was being transmitted from another world. Since that voice spoke of goodness and faith, there were those who believed it was God Almighty talking to them through the phone lines.

Almost at once, more than half of those listening—scared to death over the sins they had committed—hung up!

DEAD MAN WALKING

Fred Putnam, a shipbuilder in Maitland, Nova Scotia, was a no-nonsense businessman, and not one given to exaggeration. But to hear

Fred tell it, one would think Captain A. W. Flemming had risen from the dead, along with Flemming's wife and most of his crew.

In February 1873, Captain Flemming and fourteen crewmen, all from Great Village, Nova Scotia, sailed the *Annie Putnam* out of Maitland. They were bound for Savannah, Georgia, to discharge one cargo and load up another. Flemming had just gotten married, and—not being one who believed the old sea superstition that a woman aboard a windjammer brought bad luck—he invited his new wife along for the sail.

They ran with dirty weather for a few days, though nothing fierce; soon enough, they caught the warming benefit of the Gulf Stream current, reached the Georgia coast, and sailed the *Annie Putnam* up the Bull River to unload a cargo of deal lumber and pick up another of phosphorus rock. On their return down the Bull, a passing vessel sailed too close to the *Annie Putnam* and clipped her sails. No bad luck in that, just poor seamanship on the part of the other vessel's captain.

With the ship's rigging repaired, Captain Flemming set sail for Liverpool, England, with the cargo of phosphorus rock. Another ship sighted the *Annie Putnam* off Cape Hatteras, and that was the last those in Great Village heard about Captain Flemming, his young wife, and his crew until Lloyd's of London cabled the ship's owner, Fred Putnam: "Barque *Annie Putnam* abandoned, all lost."

No matter how long one lives by the sea, and how often bad news about a ship sinking arrives on the wind, there is no getting used to it. When Fred Putnam read the Lloyd's of London cable to the families in Great Village, the loss of loved ones cut deep.

As it turned out, the news in that cable had been slightly exaggerated.

The *Annie Putnam* had sprung a leak while in the mid-Atlantic. For three days, the crew and the donkey engine pumped like mad to keep her afloat. But phosphorus rock is highly absorbent, and it soaked up the seawater faster than the crew could pump. At last, Captain Flemming gave the order to abandon ship—and none too soon. The two lifeboats got away within minutes of the *Annie Putnam* going down.

The following day, their luck went from bad to worse. One of the lifeboats capsized, and before the crew could right it, one man had drowned.

Some may have thought it—that the woman on board had brought bad luck to ship and crew. But no one said it, especially not to Captain Flemming. It was not until the next day, when the lifeboats caught the attention of a passing yacht, that someone actually said it out loud—and that was the captain of the yacht. He coldly refused to take the shipwreck survivors aboard because he feared the presence of Mrs. Flemming.

Captain Flemming never revealed what he said to force the yacht's captain to change his mind, but it must have come with closed fists, a snarl, and more than a few threats.

A few days later, the yacht's captain breathed easier when another passing ship, the *Mary Knowlton*, responded to his signals for help and accepted all the passengers from the *Annie Putnam* without question. The *Mary Knowlton* dropped the passengers at Turks Island in the West Indies, where Governor and Mrs. Smith, the only British citizens on the island, pitied the desperation of Captain Flemming, his wife, and his crew, and welcomed them into their home. As Mrs. Smith later wrote to Mrs. Flemming: "I shall never forget how ashamed you looked the night you came to us wrapped in a table cloth."

While the crew took pleasure in the warm comfort of the island, and Mrs. Flemming in the hospitality of the governor and his wife, Captain Flemming wallowed in remorse. His spirit had gone to the bottom for the loss of the *Annie Putnam*, and of a sailor's life.

Three weeks later, a schooner bound for Halifax called at the island. It took on the shipwreck survivors, and eventually returned them home. They all checked into a Halifax hotel, where Captain Flemming anxiously plodded the hallways and lobby, feeling that he was returning home under a cloud. At last he struck out for the Halifax Club, thinking he might meet someone he knew there, someone who would understand the responsibility of taking a ship to sea, and the emptiness of heart at losing it.

Flemming entered the Halifax Club and started up the stairs— when who should be coming down but Fred Putnam.

At the sight of Captain Flemming, Putnam went as white as win- ter birch. And before Flemming could utter a word, Putnam turned on his heel and bolted back upstairs. He closed himself in the billiards room until he'd recovered his breath and speech. Then he emerged and stared at Flemming, who was leaning against the far wall with his arms folded across his chest and a hangdog look on his face.

"Good God," Fred exclaimed, "I thought you were a dead man, drowned in the Atlantic Ocean."

Captain Flemming straightened, and offered his regrets about the *Annie Putnam*.

Fred Putnam waved him off. Nothing but bad luck, Putnam said. We can all get a run of that.

Maybe so, but Mrs. Flemming never sailed with her husband again. Having a family may have had something to do with that—or maybe it was sheer superstition.

CAPTAIN EPHRAIM COOK

There are some people who live extraordinary lives, whose day-to-day doings seem to follow the big events of a region's history. One such person was Captain Ephraim Cook. He captained the *Baltimore*, one of the ships that brought 278 original settlers to Halifax in 1749. He liked what he saw, so he staked a claim on the Halifax waterfront and opened a tavern.

Captain Cook was a long-faced, adventurous, opinionated man who had little use for tavern keeping, or for the drunken, belligerent clientele he was forced to favour. In 1753, he sold the tavern to accept a commission to command a company of soldiers in protecting Nova Scotia's South Shore from French and Mi'kmaq attack. He went from serving drunk and belligerent soldiers in his tavern to leading them into battle.

In 1755, he signed on to captain a transport ship, the *Snow*, in what would become one of the most tragic displacements of an entire group of people in the history of North America: the expulsion of the Acadians from Nova Scotia.

For the next three years, Cook sailed coastal traders between Nova Scotia and New England. In 1758, Cook was back in uniform. This time he served with General Bradford's company, along with George Washington, fighting the French and Mohawk in upstate New York. At the battle of Schenectady, Cook took a musket ball to his left leg. Gangrene set in, and, without the benefit of anything stronger than a slug of rum for anaesthetic, Cook clenched his fists and bit into a hunk of rolled leather while a half-cocked surgeon sawed off his leg at the knee.

Some would despair at the loss of a leg, give in to the randomness of fate, and beg their way through a lifetime of misery. Not Ephrahim Cook. He was just getting started building a life for himself and his family. One less leg just meant he had to work harder than everyone else. And he did.

With a military pension to cover expenses, Cook sailed from Boston to Yarmouth, and was one of the original pioneers to hack homesteads out of that virgin forest. He settled at Lower Melbourne, where a beach was later named after him. He started storekeeping, and soon got up a business trading fish between Nova Scotia and New England. Then an idea hit him: process the fish in Yarmouth, and ship the processed fish into Boston and overseas to England. Like most good ideas, this one took time to catch on, but when it did, Cook had a thriving business that was sailing with a steady wind.

Others followed his lead, and before they knew it, Cook and company had on their hands the most profitable fish-processing industry in western Nova Scotia. Business now had Cook burning the candle at both ends. Nevertheless, he still took time to serve as the registrar of deeds and as a local magistrate, not to mention raising a family of eleven kids with his wife, Louisa.

Captain Ephraim Cook lived an extraordinary life, a full life with a lot of sass and daring-do. He died on November 17, 1821, and was buried on his farm in Lower Melbourne. He was eighty-one.

THE TENANTS' LEAGUE

From the time of its settlement until the last years of the nineteenth century, absentee landlords from the British Isles owned Prince Edward Island. They rented the land to farmers on the Island and hired local men to collect the rent. Most Island farmers hated the rent collectors, and in 1865, a few dozen of them banded together to resist rent payments. They called their group the Tenants' League.

For a while the league was all bluff and bluster. Then one of them hardened up his backbone and refused to pay his rent. That man was Sam Fletcher.

Sam lived near Vernon River. He was an ox for hard work, and a man who made no bones about his overwhelming dislike for the rent collectors. When he decided not to pay his rent, he went the whole hog by making a show of it.

The high sheriff of Queens County went to arrest Sam, but other members of the Tenants' League had already showed up at Sam's place as a welcoming party. They jockeyed their way between the sheriff and Sam. There was some pushing and shoving, and then Sam slid forward and landed a left hook on the sheriff's chin.

That added another charge against Sam Fletcher. On April 15, 1865, the high sheriff called for two hundred men to join a posse and ride with him to clap Sam in irons and bring him to jail. Barely fifty men turned out, and a few of them were secretly members of the Tenants' League. These few immediately sent word to Sam that the posse was coming for him.

The men had travelled a couple kilometres when the secret members of the Tenants' League claimed they were parched near to dying and begged the sheriff to stop at the Tea Hill Tavern for a round or two. The other men agreed, and the high sheriff relented.

Two rounds became three, and three made it to four. When the high sheriff and his posse finally arrived at Sam Fletcher's farm, they encountered a straw-stuffed effigy of Sam holding open the gate, and an old woman at the doorstep serving buttermilk and biscuits. That was Sam's way of telling the sheriff he was not at home.

GEORGE CORKUM

Captain George Corkum from Lunenburg, Nova Scotia, was a hard old nut with an old-fashioned way of thinking: he believed that when you got hired to do a job, you did it! In today's world, Captain Corkum would be the odd man out, an anomaly among the many who get a job and then sit back and let someone else take the helm.

In 1897, Captain Corkum had a job to do: sail the *E. P. Theriault*—a three-mast schooner owned by Archie Publicover—to the Turks and Caicos Islands with a load of lumber, then return with eleven thousand bushels of salt for the Lunenburg Outfitting Company. Other than First Mate William Snow, and Arthur Burns, a young boy making his first trip on a sailing vessel, the crew, as Corkum described them, was a gang of foreigners: warm-weather sailors from around the world.

The sail south was an easy run, with fair weather all the way. However, on reaching the Turks and Caicos, the voyage hit rock bottom. It seems the crew got into some strong Caribbean rum. When the time came to sail north, the crew refused. They wanted more rum, more women, and more time under the hot Caribbean sun.

Only two crew members were for sailing home: the Nova Scotia boys, Bill Snow and Artie Burns.

Captain Corkum barred the foreign crew from leaving the ship. But when he went to his cabin to fetch a pistol so he could force the issue, the crew jumped overboard and swam to shore. Now Corkum had a decision to make: wait in port to drum up a new crew and run a month behind schedule, or weigh anchor at once with only himself, the first mate, and a boy who barely knew the ropes to sail the *E. P. Theriault*.

A three-mast schooner is a big ship, and it takes a lot more than three hands to sail her. But as Captain Corkum said, "Three Nova Scotia sailors are worth twenty from any other place." So he set sail.

They sailed through bad weather and good, and reached Lunenburg in fifteen days—less time than the trip south.

Upon his return, Captain Corkum explained to Archie Publicover, "I had a job to do, so I did it!"

A SMALL MAN WITH
A BIG VOICE

John Hatch had a set of pipes that could be heard from one end of downtown Charlottetown to the other. He could shout down the wind and bring a bickering gaggle of wives to silence. Yelling was his job. And when he yelled, there wasn't a single soul who didn't stand to and listen. John Hatch was the town crier.

Between 1857 and 1885, he would walk the middle of the main streets in Charlottetown, ringing his big brass bell, shouting out the news of the day, and advertising whatever he had been paid to promote. In some respects, John Hatch and other town criers like him were forerunners of modern radio.

Mostly John Hatch hollered about what was on the auction block that day, charging two shillings for every item he gave attention to: a cargo of lumber, hogsheads of rum, or hampers of fancy dresses with lace on the cuffs. He had a steel-trap memory for keeping straight the goods for sale and the names of the people selling them. And there were laws about what he could say and how he had to say it. The one law John had trouble with was the one that forbade him from "crying any abusive, libellous, profane, or obscene matter or subject."

The obscene part of that law was the bit that always got John Hatch in trouble. John had a vulgar mouth. And he disliked kids. Whenever the snotty-nosed brats chased after him, making fun and hooting to disrupt his patter, John would launch a mouthful of red-rag that blistered with obscenity. His preferred words were always the worse ones.

He lived alone for most of his life. Then in 1877, he married a Newfoundland woman. She had a son who she renamed after her new husband. Maybe it was Hatch's wife who softened his hard-heartedness, or maybe it was the boy who fulfilled an old man's long desire for family. However it was, John Hatch took to young Johnny, and the two became such good friends they were seldom apart.

When Hatch went blind in 1880, his job was on the line. How could a blind man be the town crier? the mayor and council asked.

Young Johnny showed them how. He led his father through the streets of town, ringing the bell and prompting his old man with what to say. Old John Hatch may have lost his sight, but he still had pipes that could rattle windows and unlock doors. But although he was more even tempered than he had ever been, the kids still mocked him from behind, and he still coloured the air a dark shade of blue.

For thirty years, John Hatch bellowed through the Charlottetown streets. He died in 1885. He was eighty years old.

JIMMY PADDY MCGUINESS

With the outbreak of the First World War, convicts in Dorchester Penitentiary got the chance to serve in the front line for their freedom. Jimmy Paddy McGuiness was one of the first to volunteer. He was in jail for manslaughter. He'd accidentally killed a man in a scrap down in Rolla Bay, Prince Edward Island—a crime he deeply regretted.

He served well in the war. In 1916, he took a bullet in the chest, a severe wound that sent him home to PEI—as a free man.

McGuiness was quick with figures. It was said he could measure lumber at a glance and work out the most complicated math problems in his head.

In 1917, the east end of PEI needed a schoolteacher. Despite his past, McGuiness applied for and got the job. However, when he arrived at school, he had few students to teach. That was the year of the great flu epidemic—the Spanish flu. People on the Island were dying left and right. Whole families were wiped out.

There was no back and forth visiting that year, and certainly no going to school. Frightened of the epidemic, people kept to themselves. Entire families were bedridden, many unable to get groceries, bring in wood, or cook a meal and feed themselves.

McGuiness saw that he had a job to do, and something he could teach. He went door to door firing stoves, feeding the hungry, and caring for the sick and dying. He risked his life on the back roads of Prince Edward Island the way he had risked his life in the front lines of the First World War. Jimmy Paddy McGuiness gave back to the people who had taken a chance on him and were open-minded enough to forgive his past.

TAPPAN ADNEY

(BJG)

By the time he settled in Woodstock, New Brunswick, Tappan Adney was a New York journalist who had already lived the adventurous life most of us only dream of. He had covered the story of the Klondike Gold Rush in the 1860s by sharing the lode with the original sourdoughs. He had climbed the treacherous Chilkoot Pass and roughed it for two years while panning for gold. When he returned east, he published *The Great Stampede*, the best title out of scores of books on the gold rush.

Sixty-four years later, Pierre Berton turned out his first bestseller, called *Klondike*. The difference between Berton's book and Adney's is that Berton wrote about what he had researched; Adney wrote about what he had done.

Years later, Adney made his adventurous way to Woodstock and took out Canadian citizenship. He went overseas with the Canadian Forces in 1916, and returned as a lieutenant of engineers.

After the war, he climbed in the Andes, shared a New York apartment with poet Bliss Carman, and became a fine photographer and an excellent graphic artist. The rest of his time, he spent among Native people. It was said that he became one of the only three English-speaking white men to master Maliseet, the language of the First Peoples of the St. John River Valley.

But his real interest was birchbark canoes. First he learned from the Maliseet how to build them. Then he built scores of them. Then he wrote about building them, and his book is still kept at the Smithsonian Institute as the definitive work on the subject.

By the time he died in 1950, Tappan Adney had lived the lives of half a dozen men all rolled into one.

UNSUNG HEROES

The year is 1896. Robert Otterson from Truro, Nova Scotia, was a sailor aboard the *Kings County*, a passenger ship sailing between Antwerp and New York. Also on board was John Porter, a sea captain by trade, but on this crossing, John Porter was just another passenger.

John Porter had sailed to Europe six months before, met a young woman, and married her. He and his bride were on their way home by way of New York, where they planned to honeymoon.

Midway across the Atlantic, one of the forty passengers took a fever and developed pustules on the skin. Then a sailor developed the same. Another passenger became stricken. And another. Within days, all four had died.

The passengers and crew panicked. And there was no one to maintain order, because the captain now lay in his cabin dying of the same disease: smallpox.

Robert Otterson saw the crew in confusion and quickly took command. He knew John Porter was an experienced sea captain, and asked Porter to captain the ship to New York. Then Otterson rolled up his sleeves and tended to those suffering from the dreaded and highly infectious disease.

Suddenly at his side was the young bride, Mrs. Porter, ready to risk her life to nurse the sick and dying. Together they saved nearly a dozen lives.

In New York, the ship was quarantined. But not before Otterson slipped Captain and Mrs. Porter over the side onto Staten Island, so they could honeymoon without the intrusion of New York doctors and newspapermen.

LOFTUS FORTIER AND A THREE-POUND KEY

In 1710, Francis Nicholson and Samuel Vetch led an army of New England soldiers into Acadie—now Nova Scotia—to capture the French outpost of Port Royal. They surrounded the fort and riddled the walls with grapeshot and musket fire.

The French garrison bravely withstood the siege, but soon their nerves and provisions gave out, and they surrendered. The actual surrender was a formal and symbolic affair in which the French ceremoniously marched from Port Royal and passed a large iron key over to Francis Nicholson. The key was nine inches long and weighed three pounds. It fit the large iron lock on the door to Port Royal.

Nicholson returned to Boston and took the key with him. The British changed the name of Port Royal to Annapolis Royal, and the name of the fort there to Fort Anne. Over the years and centuries, the settlement grew and prospered.

Between 1917 and 1933, Loftus Fortier mapped out and measured pretty close to every square foot of the ditch and earthworks of old Fort Anne. He knew the casemates inch by inch, as well as the ironstone walls, the dungeon, the powder magazine, and the brick and timber of the officers' quarters. He knew when to duck below a sagging beam and when to sidestep a soft plank. He knew where the cobbles on the path to the beach were loose underfoot, and where the chink in the arch of the sally port had crumbled away.

Loftus Fortier was born in Kingston, Ontario, in 1858. He served in the immigration branch of the Canadian department of the interior, first in Ottawa and then, in 1893, in Winnipeg. It was not until 1913 that Loftus Fortier boarded the train east to close out his career as a civil servant in Annapolis Royal, Nova Scotia. He rode against the westward spread of people, against the turn of time. Rode through the coal smoke bending back over the cars. He rode into a dream of living in a town that had been one of the first founded in North America, a dream of living in the long ago.

At station stops and from the darkness of the railway car, he watched car knockers step through steam carrying oil cans and lanterns. They hammered ice from steam hitches that connected the pipes that delivered heat to the passenger cars, and highballed their lights for the train to roll ahead. Slow on the get-go like an ant lugging a dead worm. Gathering speed.

Soon he lost his thoughts to the train's steady beat on the rails, to the sweep of level land heaving with the cold. Snow banked against the houses and barns for warmth, and against the railway shanties along the tracks.

Loftus Fortier settled into a quiet life as a civil servant in Annapolis Royal. Then in 1917, he started digging at the ruins of old Fort Anne as a way of digging grief from his own heart, a way of burying the unburied bones of his son who had been killed in the Great War. He dug alongside archaeologists from Ottawa and Halifax. He dug during the off hours from his posting as inspector of agencies with the immigration branch of the department of the interior. After he retired in 1920, he dug every chance he got. He unearthed the tragic history of this place. He filled birch baskets with soil damp with the tears of more than two hundred years of back and forth killing. Dead soldiers, French and English, most of them not much older than his own son, ordered to war by the same soulless men who later signed the peace. The clots of their lives seemed to stick to his shovel. And still he dug. It was almost as though the more he unearthed of that old fort—the stone walls, the brass cannon, the mill wheel, the iron shot, the button off a soldier's tunic—the more he understood that history is eternal, and that each life, with its own particular memories, is redeemable.

Later, after his heart had healed, his digging became a way of digging beyond his own self, a way of shovelling through his fifty-nine years and smoke-drawn memories into something more eternal than his own life.

In the mid-1920s, Loftus Fortier excited his neighbours and friends in Annapolis Royal to help him turn the Fort Anne ruins into a museum. Together they swept away two hundred years of dust and scrubbed off an equal amount of mould from the officer's barracks. They preserved what they could from the past and showed it without showing off, the way a doily accents the plainness of a pitcher or a pot of tea. What had once been the crumble of a forgotten past had become the centrepiece for civic pride.

Often Fortier guided tourists himself from one exhibit to the next. For him the past lived in the dust and silence of the glass-cased artefacts and in the crust of tarnish on the brass cannon. With each tour he seemed to slip through a crack between one moment and the next to imagine himself in the long ago. He spoke of soldiers as though he knew them. He described battles as though he himself had been there. He poked at the earthworks as though his own blood had dampened them. He fingered stonewalls as though he had once pressed against them in fear.

At the main gate, his eyes would fill to tell of the French surrender in 1710, when Subercase, the French commander, had paraded his garrison from the fort with more ceremony than his defeated soldiers deserved. And then Fortier's face would lengthen just at the thought of Colonel Francis Nicholson and Samuel Vetch, accepting the key to the fort, and then the British letting it fall to ruin. He mourned the death of this fort as though it were his child. He always concluded his remarks by saying it was most unfortunate the key to the main gate had been lost to history.

Among one group of visitors were four members of the Massachusetts Historical Society. They viewed the museum display and ruins of the old fort, and listened to Fortier's tale with interest. The following year they returned to Annapolis Royal and presented Loftus Fortier with a gift—an object that had been in their possession for a long time—a large iron key, nine inches long and weighing three pounds.

Fortier could not have been happier. It was as though the Massachusetts visitors had given him the missing piece to life's puzzle.

On June 22, 1933, Loftus Fortier walked the path from Annapolis Royal and into the fort. He tapped his cane steady on the loose cobbles and held tight to his straw boater against the strong wind off the Basin. His cream-colored suit fell baggy with his loss of weight. Dust kicked up on his black shoes. He selected a bench overlooking the Basin and settled himself to listen to the

First Regimental Band strike up its opening number for the first concert of the summer season.

His well-wishers were many. Several joined him on the bench and on the grass at his feet. Fortier listened contentedly to the music and to the conversation and to the wind and the gulls and the ripple of the waves. For Loftus Fortier, it was a seamless pattern of sounds. A song. The way moments make a life.

He died that day listening to the music. He was seventy-five.

MARRIAGES

(BJG)

Today, premarital sex among young adults is common; with some, it's almost a foregone conclusion. But in an earlier era, "trying each other out" was not only frowned upon, it was illegal—unless the couple were "bundling" with their parents' consent.

Bundling was an ancient custom originating in England. Typically, a girl's parents let her sleep one night with the lad courting her. If the pair decided they were suited, they soon married; if not, they parted forever—unless she later proved pregnant. Then the lad *had* to wed her, or be tarred and feathered...or worse.

One evening in 1770, Captain William Owen of the Royal Navy anchored near one of the Cranberry Islands off the coast of Maine—then a part of Massachusetts. His pilot, Aaron Bunker, had barely gone ashore when he came roaring back. He'd discovered his sister Mary in bed with Eliachim Eaton of Deer Island, New Brunswick, and he was fit to kill. He didn't care that they were bundling with their parents' permission. As far as Bunker was concerned, the couple was making the beast with two backs, and to him that was a disgrace to his family name. He swore that if the captain didn't come ashore and wed the couple, he'd slit Eaton's throat.

Captain Owen gave in.

To complicate things, another island couple had recently been wed by the skipper of a small schooner called the *Dolphin*, but they were afraid their marriage hadn't taken, because the *Dolphin* was a small ship and its captain was a nobody.

Captain Owen, on the other hand, was an important man—and wealthy. Four years earlier, King George III had granted all of Campobello Island to Owen, and these islanders trusted his powers.

To preserve the peace, satisfy the Bunker family's honour, and reassure the uncertain, Captain Owen went ashore the next morning. He married Eliachim Eaton to Mary Bunker, and remarried Robert McLellan to Jerusha Frost.

Communal joy and a feast followed, and, as Owen wrote in his diary, "a real and general Yankee frolic ensued."

BLACKFISH CHOLERA

Walk among the headstones in the Hantsport Cemetery, and you'll notice a number of those buried there died in the summer of 1888. Death did not come to their homes like a thief in the night—no, indeed. There was no sneaking around this time. Death came to the picturesque town of Hantsport on the Avon River like a stern-wheeler blasting its horn for all to run down to the shore and have a look. And what folks saw that summer morning in 1888 was a mess of black fish washed up on the riverbank.

There were hundreds of them—one man said thousands—and they covered the shoreline like a massive, black, puke-stinking carpet. The stench carried as far away as Windsor.

A town meeting brought forth the suggestion that the fish should not go to waste: that they should be cut up and used as fertilizer on the apple orchards. So farmers and townsfolk went to work cutting, hauling, and spreading.

A few weeks later, some townsfolk and farmers came down with severe diarrhea and stomach cramps. Then others caught them too. Before long, all three hundred families in the town of Hantsport had reported at least one case of the sickness. People now suffered from violent vomiting, diarrhea, and aching muscles and joints. Some were worse, much worse, with sunken eyes, hollow cheeks, dry skin, and blood circulation that had almost stopped. It was like their insides had dissolved into mush, with their bodies shivering on the outside and burning up within.

Dr. C. I. Margeson, the only physician in Hantsport at that time, recognized the disease characteristics as an epidemic of cholera. He and Reverend James McLean rolled up their sleeves and spent day and night ministering to the sick by pumping liquids into them orally and intravenously.

Medical treatment for cholera had come a long way since an earlier epidemic in Halifax in 1834. Then, the wealthier sort quickly packed their bags and left town, but not before voting for a meagre five British pounds "to relieve the distress of the Poor during this time of direful calamity." Those left behind burned tar barrels that were strategically placed about the town. The fires burned day and night. People congregated around them, believing in the curing ability of their "powerful purifying vapours."

Years later, in 1866, Halifax authorities had feared another outbreak of the disease, and so designated Hugonins Point on McNabs Island as a quarantine station to handle the cholera-infected passengers aboard an immigrant ship, the S. S. *England*. At that time, authorities still believed that cholera spread on noxious vapours that emanated from the infected. Police and the military patrolled the waters around McNabs Island to keep the 1,200 passengers from crossing into Halifax. And once again, those who possessed the means to do so hightailed it out of town.

It took guts, dedication, and a deep-seated belief in God's promise of a heavenly afterlife for Dr. John Stayner, as well as a Roman Catholic priest and three Sisters of Charity, to tend the sick and dying for days on end, and in extremely unhealthy circumstances

More than two hundred people died on McNabs Island in 1866. Dr. John Stayner was among them.

Despite the advancement in medical science that had identified contaminated food and water as the source of cholera, most people in 1888—including medical practitioners—still feared its transmission from person to person through airborne vapours. In rural Hantsport, with family and neighbours suddenly bloating up, vomiting violently, and squirting their bowels through the eye of a needle, people were scared to leave their homes. It took more than an average supply of courage for Dr. Margeson and Reverend McLean to go among the infected to feed them water and soothe their suffering.

Forty-six died in Hansport before health authorities identified the source of the epidemic as the decaying black fish—among them the town's undertaker, John Borden. It was now necessary to get rid of the disease-ridden fish. That sorry lot fell onto the shoulders of Judson Pulsifer.

If Doc Margeson and Reverend McLean were brave to tend to the sickly, Judson Pulsifer was damn near saintly to shovel the cholera-contaminated fish into barrels, load the barrels onto wagons, and haul them to Simmon's Hill near the Mount Denson Bridge, where he buried them in deep trenches. He then hauled lime from Churchill's quarry to the trenches, and shovelled that onto the fetid fish. Last of all, he filled in the trenches with dirt, then went home and waited for his own body to bloat up with cholera. No one had been more exposed to this dreaded disease than Judson Pulsifer.

For more than a week afterwards, he lived a very lonely life, as his family and neighbours avoided his company. He ate meals alone, slept alone, and whenever he went out for a stroll, he pretty much had the streets to himself. Soon enough, it became clear that Judson Pulsifer was not getting sick, and that had folks figuring that either he had stepped in a healthy pile of good luck, or the Lord's most trusted angel had taken him under its wing.

After that, it was backslaps and a chorus of "thank yous," as the people of Hantsport—and others for kilometres around—realized they owed their health to three brave men: Doc Margeson, Reverend McLean, and Judson Pulsifer.

THE FLOATING DANCE HALL

The orchestra played popular tunes for the year 1900 as high-stepping strutters showed their stuff in this floating dance hall. The hall was lavishly festooned with coloured crepe, a mirror ball, and the latest rage: Chinese lanterns suspended from the ceiling and from thick wooden posts. None of those attending this midsummer dance on Shediac Bay would have ever guessed the boards they were dancing on had once been soaked with human blood.

Captain Charles Nash and his pretty wife had lived aboard the *Henry Fuller*, a 175-foot barquentine that traded between the Maritimes and the Boston States. Captain Nash was an unusually quiet man for a sea captain. For him, fifty words a day was a mouthful. His wife was as taciturn and reserved as her husband.

The crew consisted of a hard-weather, whiskey-drinking man named Thomas Bram, who was the first mate, and two no-account deckhands, Banberg and Monk. Jonathan Spencer, a black man, was steward to the captain and his wife.

On the night of July 14, 1896, the *Henry Fuller* was mid-sail between Boston and Halifax. Banberg had the watch until midnight, when Bram relieved him. Monk was at the helm, and before Bram came on deck, Monk heard the captain scold Bram for his drinking.

Just before two o'clock in the morning, Monk heard a woman scream. He went to the forecastle to fetch his revolver, then headed straight for Mrs. Nash's room, where he saw a sight that sickened him on the spot: her body stretched on the floor, all bloody and horribly mutilated.

Monk reeled backwards into the chartroom—and there he found the captain lying on the floor with his skull cleaved in two. In the next moment, Spencer was at Monk's side, having also responded—though a little late—to Mrs. Nash's scream. As Spencer stood over the captain's body, his knees wobbled and his mouth filled with stomach suck. He swallowed and gagged, then readied himself for what Monk said he would see in Mrs. Nash's room.

Spencer thought of mutiny right away, and armed himself with the captain's revolver. Then he and Monk went on deck, where Bram was still keeping watch.

Bram had a revolver stuck in his belt, as though he already knew what Spencer and Monk were about to tell him. When Spencer asked about Banberg, Bram shook his head and shrugged. Then Spencer entered the forecastle and found Banberg dead in his bunk with his head split in two. Not far away, in a corner of the forecastle, was the bloody axe.

The three men now stood on deck of that square-rigged vessel with revolvers in their hands and suspicion in their eyes. At least one of them had to be a maniac and an axe murderer.

Despite Bram's rank of first mate, Spencer—a strong-willed individual, perhaps from years of tutelage under Captain Nash—assumed control of the ship, took the helm, and set a course for Halifax. Needless to say, he did not sleep that night. Neither did the others.

The following morning, Bram suggested they throw the stinking bodies overboard. Spencer thought otherwise. Battling nausea, he and Monk, with their pistols well within reach, sewed the bodies inside canvas sheets and respectfully laid them in the tender that was towed behind the *Henry Fuller*.

They were six more days and nights of sailing ahead, and still Spencer stayed awake at the helm, his body shaking from lack of sleep and his nerves shot from sheer terror. Monk helped in the rigging, and kept watch in the bow at night. Twice he fell asleep leaning against the foremast, and twice he woke in panic, waving his pistol at nothing.

Bram did little to help. Mostly he sat on deck with his back to the forecastle, his eyes cocked on Spencer, and his fingers curled around his pistol-grip.

The *Henry Fuller* reached Halifax on July 20, without further incident. The Halifax authorities arrested all three men for mutiny and sent them to Boston, the ship's homeport, for trial.

Having assumed command and sailed for Halifax served Spencer well in the eyes of the court. Monk received the same benefit for his role in caring for the dead, and for helping Spencer sail the ship. Bram's behaviour, on the other hand, roused suspicion, but suspicion was not enough for an easy conviction. Without an independent eyewitness, any one of the men could have murdered the captain, Mrs. Nash, and Banberg, and that weighed heavily on the jury.

After thirty-one ballots, the twelve men finally reached a decision: that Thomas Bram had acted alone in committing the murders.

And yet, despite the barbarity of the crime, a nagging doubt prevented the judge from exacting the full measure of the law: the gallows. Instead, he sentenced Thomas Bram to life in prison.

As for the *Henry Fuller*, it sold at public auction for a pittance. The gruesome murders may have had something to do with that, or it could have been the slump in international trade at the time, or the changeover to steel-hulled ships. Whatever it was that devalued the *Henry Fuller*, one New Brunswicker didn't care. He hollered out the highest bid at auction, and, after sailing the ship to Halifax and then New Brunswick, he turned that death ship into a floating dance hall on Shediac Bay.

DISRESPECT

Members of provincial legislatures think a lot of themselves, but none more so than those in the legislature at Charlottetown, Prince Edward Island, during the eighteenth century. Members of that legislature engaged in highfalutin displays of self-importance. They strutted the streets of Charlottetown and the halls of government dressed in scarlet cloaks, gold lace, and hats with huge feather plumes that draped over their heads and down their backs. They were as pompous as peacocks.

One day, Captain MacDonald told them so. MacDonald was a Scots Highlander who lived out around Tracadie. Seeing the legislature's grandiose display just once was more than enough for MacDonald. He let loose a slew of galling insults, and the legislature members turned as scarlet as their cloaks.

The legislature decided it was entitled to ordinary respect from the lesser sort, and sent the sergeant-at-arms to bring MacDonald before the House for a reprimand.

The sergeant-at-arms followed MacDonald along the twenty kilometres to Tracadie. There he found MacDonald living the life of an independent highland chieftain, surrounded by hundreds of his clansmen.

MacDonald scoffed at the order to appear before the House. "Tell those you serve that if they again send a messenger here, I'll send a score of my men to drive the bunch of them (Lords, Commons, and Councillors) into a big cellar under a barn, where they can make laws for the animals."

The sergeant-at-arms delivered the message to the legislature. There was a flurry of commotion, a lot of squawking and flapping. Then the legislature decided that MacDonald's appearance was not necessary. "It would only give him importance," said one member.

And so, they bravely and unanimously resolved to ignore MacDonald's insults.

BAD LUCK

Some people have all the luck, and others have none. No matter what the lucky ones attempt to do, they succeed. Others—the people who don't have any lucky bones in their bodies—could attempt a simple task with all the odds in their favour and still fall short. Their best-laid plans never seem to work out exactly as they envisioned.

Take John Gill, for instance, a man born on the wrong side of the blanket. At the outbreak of the American Revolution, he had a choice between the rebels and the Loyalists. He chose the Loyalists.

John Gill's choice had nothing to do with politics, or whether or not he believed in king and country. He just wanted to be on the winning side and reap the harvest that came with victory. Instead, he caught the losing end of the stick, and had to forfeit what little he owned to the victorious rebels and board a transport ship for Halifax, Nova Scotia. Poor choice, some might say, but others would see it as a stroke of bad luck.

John Gill landed in Halifax with little more than the shirt on his back, and grew poorer with every passing day. There were moments during any given day that might show promise, but by the time the night watch called "curfew" and John rolled into the rack, the promise he had pinned his hopes on had turned, as it always did, into disappointment and regret.

For example, on March 29, 1787, at four o'clock in the afternoon, John Gill walked past Godfried Schwartz's dry goods store in Halifax, and noticed that Schwartz was not in the front room. To Gill's mind, the situation showed promise. But the promise demanded action, immediate action.

Without a second thought, John carefully slipped into Schwartz's store, and, without looking around, quickly ducked behind the counter and stuffed nine silk handkerchiefs into the pockets of his greatcoat. He heard Schwartz still fussing about in the backroom, and so he reached for a silver watch and pocketed that too.

As he slid back around the counter to make his escape, his promise of good luck suddenly went from damp to dry. There, staring him in the face, was Captain Alexander McCullough.

McCullough was an army officer, a big man with big hands that snapped out and grabbed John Gill by the collar. If there was one thing Captain McCullough hated more than a cowardly soldier, it was a thief. He shook John Gill silly then turned him over to a local magistrate, who just happened to have been standing behind the open door the whole time John Gill was sneaking into the store, nipping behind the counter, and pocketing his booty. This man was Anthony Stewart, a justice of the peace.

At John Gill's trial, on Tuesday, November 6, 1787, McCullough and Stewart testified to what they had witnessed in Schwartz's dry goods store. Then, without much discussion, the jury reached a verdict. Robert Carroll, the jury foreman, rose in the jury box to declare Gill guilty of breaking into Godfried Schwartz's store and stealing nine silk handkerchiefs and one silver watch.

The judge then ordered the bailiff to examine the prisoner's hands. This is where John Gill's luck plummeted right through the bottom.

In the fat of Gill's left thumb was a branded scar of the letter *T* for thief. It turned out that in October 1786, Gill and an accomplice—a fellow named John Anderson—had broken into a waterfront warehouse and stolen a hamper of women's clothes. As luck would have it, Gill and Anderson had cleared the warehouse cleanly, then turned into an alley and run smack into two magistrates on night watch duty.

The judge who presided over the trial for the warehouse theft had been lenient on Gill, sentencing him to the branding on his left thumb. Gill had been given a choice by that judge: go straight or face the consequences. John Gill chose wrong.

Breaking into Schwartz's store was John's second conviction for theft. Without having to hear the sentence, John already knew what the judge would say.

That afternoon, at one o'clock, John climbed the gallows and, without a single word spoken on his behalf, the hangman brought an end to John Gill's stretch of bad luck.

POISON GAS

On April 22, 1915, at the battle of Ypres, the Germans introduced gas warfare during World War One. As the war progressed, so did the production of the gas, as well as deadly improvements to its potency. By 1917, both sides of the war were manufacturing mortar shells filled with mustard gas, also called Yperite. Gas warfare killed nearly one hundred thousand soldiers and civilians during that war, and permanently injured more than a million.

During the Second World War, the Allies had every reason to believe the Germans would use gas warfare again. This time, the Allies were ready for it.

In the winter of 1942, a convoy left Halifax with supplies and munitions for the Allied war effort in Europe. Aircraft could protect the convoy only as far as their limited supply of fuel would allow. After the planes turned back, the convoy entered the "Black Pit," an area outside the range of air cover where German U-boats lay in wait. Allied battleships, destroyers, and corvettes provided some limited protection. One of the escort ships for this convoy was the corvette *Minas*.

No sooner had the convoy entered the Black Pit than a U-boat broke the surface and fired two torpedoes. A merchant ship caught one of the torpedoes in the bow and the other at midship. The crew hardly had time to jump overboard into the immense dark of that vast ocean.

The *Minas* steamed to the rescue, battling the high sea to drag nearly a dozen men out of the freezing water. Within minutes, the corvette's crew had the coughing, choking survivors below deck, wrapped in blankets and sipping mugs of hot soup. Suddenly, and almost all at once, the merchant sailors began coughing uncontrollably and struggling for a breath. They became delirious, and within minutes, half a dozen were dead.

At first the corvette's crew thought those six survivors had gone hypothermic and died. Then the other six survivors began to struggle for breath. Finally, from the last of the survivors, the crew of the *Minas* learned what the merchant ship had been carrying: poison gas, destined for a storage facility in the United Kingdom.

For all their effort to rescue the twelve sailors from the winter sea, the corvette's crew had only corpses to show for it—and the frightening knowledge that their own side was preparing to engage in gas warfare.

CAVALIERS

AND

SCALLYWAGS

LANGUAGE AND HABIT

Moses Grass was born in Waasis, a backwoods community in central New Brunswick, in 1865. "Mosey" was a bit simple-minded. When his first wife died, he couldn't properly feed and clothe the family of youngsters that was now his sole responsibility. The children foraged the neighbourhood to find enough to eat and wear, and in the 1920s, one of them—a lad of eight years—wandered the eleven kilometres into Fredericton.

At the time, Reverend Earl McKnight was pastor of the George Street Baptist Church. He and his wife were kindly people. They learned of the Grass child's plight and took him into their home. Young Grass was basically a good boy, and he was bright, but he brought with him something he'd learned at home: a vocabulary of blasphemy and vulgarity that would make a stevedore blush.

The McKnights were patient. For several weeks, they asked him, then pleaded with him, then charged him strongly to stop using such dreadful words. Nothing worked. Their sensibilities worn thin and their Christian fortitude all but exhausted, they decided Grass would have to go.

One morning, Mrs. McKnight packed a lunch and a small bag of clothes, and told the boy he had to find another place to stay. With her last words, she warned him not to use bad language. Then she closed the door on the little fellow and breathed a sigh—a mixture of regret and relief.

The next twelve hours of the McKnights' day passed uneventfully. Then, about eight o'clock in the evening, there was a knock at their door. There at the threshold stood the same forlorn lad.

"And what did you do?" Mrs. McKnight asked.

"Well," said young Grass, "I went all the way up one side a' them long roads, an' all the way down the other. An' they wasn't a goddamn one a' them would take me in."

Mrs. McKnight shook her head and held open the door.

ABEL'S CAPE

Abel's Cape, in Fortune Bay, Prince Edward Island, takes its name from Edward Abel, a land agent who collected rents from the tenant farmers. Abel worked for Lord Townshend, an Englishman and an absentee landlord.

Most of Prince Edward Island's early settlers were tenant farmers, working their muscles and bones for someone else's benefit. And if they equated anyone with the off-scouring of hell, it was the absentee landlord and his henchman—the rent collector.

Edward Abel had a snarling, disquieting disposition. His wife was even worse. She was a mean-spirited, spiteful woman who ran ice water in her veins instead of blood, and lorded her uppity self over those her husband collected from. On top of that, she had a bullying way of getting whatever she wanted.

In 1819, she hankered for a black carriage horse owned by a tenant farmer named Pat Pearse. When she heard Pat had turned in a poor crop that year and was hurting for cash, she insisted her husband demand rent money from him at once.

Pat turned out his pockets to show Edward he couldn't pay. So Edward Abel, on his wife's suggestion, offered to take Pat's black horse as payment.

That horse was prize breeding stock, and Pat Pearse's only chance for making a go of it on his plot of ground. Pat turned down Abel's offer, and went begging rent money from his friends and neighbours.

Abel's wife took a fit, raging against her husband, the tenants, and all that was holy. She refused the money. She said some of the coins were Spanish, and therefore worthless, and threw them in Pat Pearse's face.

Pat again made the rounds to his neighbours, changing the Spanish coins for English. When he returned home, he saw Edward Abel with a bridle on the prize horse, leading it from the stable.

Now it was Pat's turn to go red with rage. He rushed into his house, and returned to the farmyard carrying an old musket with a bayonet attached. When Edward Abel refused to drop the bridle, Pat stabbed him seven times in the arms and groin.

Abel lived long enough to tell his wife what had happened, and she put a price of fifty pounds on Pat Pearse's head. But there were no takers. Most of those around Fortune Bay figured Pat had done what they had long wanted to do, and they hid Pat whenever the authorities came looking.

For five years, Pat Pearse lived on the run, splitting the countryside on his prize black horse. During all that time, the Abel woman boiled with the desire for revenge. Some say that's what eventually killed her: a calloused heart bloated with hate. After her death, Pat came out of hiding, and that probably had her rolling over in her grave.

SAM NAPIER

Samuel Hawkins Napier had big dreams and empty pockets, though for one short stretch of his life, he was the cock of the walk in New Brunswick.

Sam was born in Scotland in 1837. He later immigrated with his family to Bonaventure, Quebec, and then, when he was seven years old, settled in Bathurst, New Brunswick. In the 1850s, gold was the talk of the town—Australian gold. Soon enough, Sam's older brother, Charles, struck out for the goldfields on the far side of the globe.

It didn't take Sam long to chase after the same dream. In 1857, he worked his passage to Australia aboard the clipper ship *Marco Polo*. The brothers partnered in a claim on the goldfield in Kingower, Victoria. Within a few months, they struck it rich by digging up the largest gold nugget ever discovered. It weighed upwards of fifty-seven kilograms, and a replica of it is still kept at the British Museum.

The Napier brothers sold the giant nugget to the Bank of England for sixty thousand dollars, which would be in the millions today. They split the take, and Charles returned to Australia to live the life of Riley, while Sam sailed home to Bathurst, where he lived high as well—maybe a little too high.

Sam went through his money as though life was nothing but flowers and frolics. And he had hangers-on who tapped his money supply, the kind of men who pissed more than they drank. They bragged up Sam like he was some conquering hero who had returned to New Brunswick to walk among the lesser sort. They soon talked him into running for the provincial legislature.

Sam, however, was no ordinary politician. He had seen more of the world than the Miramichi and St. John River Valleys, and he had learned early on that life is a short and crooked road that a fellow must laugh at and drink to at every turn. So when he settled behind his desk in the New Brunswick legislature, he did so with a larky smile and a wild, almost reckless manner that riled John S. Covert, the stiff-necked Liberal member sitting opposite him.

One day, when Covert was scheduled to speak in an important debate, Sam entered the legislature with a mysterious parcel, which he quickly stuffed inside his desk. When Covert rose to address the chamber, Sam opened the lid of his desk and poked at the thing inside, and that brought angry crowing from the desk which silenced Covert in mid-sentence.

All eyes snapped to Sam Napier, who sat with a boyish look of innocence on his face. Then Covert began to speak again.

This time, Sam threw his desk wide open. Inside was a rooster, which screeched and cock-a-doodled and beat its wings frantically. It jumped from Sam's desk to the next one over, and then to one desk after another, flapping and squawking, all the while pursued by the clerk of the House, the sergeant-at-arms, and many of the members.

The House was bedlam for nearly an hour. At last, they caught the bird and removed it from the chamber. Covert again rose to speak, but his words were lost to the continuous laughter from both sides.

On another occasion when Covert rose to speak, an Italian organ grinder, standing outside the legislature, filled the chamber with the most strident, melancholic music anyone there had ever heard.

Covert stopped speaking and stared at Sam, who sat with his chair tipped back on its hind legs, smiling that larky smile of his.

Sam soon gave up politics. He lost much of his money in failed business ventures, and blew the rest. In 1896, he hopped a train to Ottawa, where he worked for a logging company in Gatineau, Quebec. For all the friends Sam Napier had when he was rich, he died alone and penniless, in a small cabin on the outskirts of nowhere.

FREDERICTON DUEL

(BJG)

Early in 1800, a black woman named Nancy hauled Captain Caleb Jones into court, determined to break his claim of ownership over her. Nancy was a slave, and Jones was a miserable master. He beat her unmercifully, and she figured that was good cause for the court to force him to give her up.

Seven of the best lawyers in New Brunswick gathered there. Five of them, including John Murray Bliss, took Captain Jones's side, while Ward Chipman and Samuel Denny-Lee Street stood for Nancy.

Long before the legal arguments ended, tempers flared white-hot. After one tempestuous exchange, Bliss declared he'd been insulted by Samuel Denny-Lee Street and challenged the opposing lawyer to a duel.

Stair Agnew stood as second for Bliss; a Mr. Anderson was second for Street. They gathered in the courthouse yard. Agnew, who loaded the pistols, suggested that if the first shots had no effect, the affair should end. But Street objected. He said that no second had the right to measure out satisfaction for *him*. He insisted on reloads.

The seconds measured off the distance—nine paces—and again Street protested: he wanted to get closer, but the seconds refused his request. The signal went up. The pistols roared. And when the smoke cleared, Bliss and Street were as healthy as they'd ever been.

Street demanded another go. But before the guns could be reloaded, Anderson hurried over to Bliss and said that if Bliss had not meant any *personal* insult during the court argument, that would be enough to settle the row. Bliss nodded.

Word of Bliss's agreement passed back to Street, and, as Anderson's account says, "Street very handsomely acceded and the gentlemen parted apparently good friends."

And by the way—Nancy won her freedom.

AMERICAN PRIVATEERS

New England fishermen were the original settlers of Liverpool, Nova Scotia. Many had been fishing those Nova Scotia waters for years, and settling in Liverpool just got them closer to the best places to fish.

Because of their New England heritage, many of the Liverpool settlers supported the American Revolution against Great Britain. This raised tensions in the port town. There was a lot of arguing and some fist fighting, and once or twice a pistol was drawn in the name of King George or for the sake of American liberty.

All that changed when American privateers started raiding Liverpool ships. These American sailors raided first and asked questions later. And those in Liverpool who had supported the Americans changed their minds when they started losing money to what they now called "Yankee pirates."

So in 1776, when an American privateer attacked Liverpool and captured Fort Morris, most of the Liverpool settlers volunteered for the local militia. They rallied on the waterfront behind Colonel Simeon Perkins's warehouse. With muskets and cannons, they attacked the Americans, and within a few hours they had recaptured Fort Morris.

That settled the argument in Liverpool once and for all. From that day on, Liverpool was for King George, and anyone who said otherwise was not welcome in the town.

Colonel Perkins later petitioned the Halifax government for a company of British soldiers to help protect the harbour, and the following year, Perkins outfitted a Liverpool ship manned by Liverpool sailors. Over the next few years, the ship sailed the American coast, giving back to the Americans what they had been dishing out.

PIERRE MARTIN

The Maliseet in Northumberland County, New Brunswick, sided with the Americans against the British during the American

Revolution. Many Maliseet warriors had fought with the French twenty years before at Fort Beausejour, and later in Quebec on the Plains of Abraham. Now, in the 1770s, English settlers were claiming land in Northumberland County as theirs, and this gave the Maliseet a common cause with the Americans.

The English responded. In 1777, Captain Harvey of the British sloop *Viper* attacked and captured an American privateer, the *Layfayette*. Harvey crewed the *Layfayette* with British sailors and marines, but continued to fly American colours. He then enlisted the support of Mr. Ross, a well-known salt merchant. With Ross on board, Captain Harvey wanted the Maliseet to think the *Layfayette* was an American trading ship.

The ruse worked. Thirty Maliseet warriors came on board, and all were immediately clapped in irons—all except one, Pierre Martin, a barrel-chested man who had a heart swollen with courage.

Martin took two marines and crushed them in his arms, then swung their lifeless bodies like clubs, fighting his way across the deck to free his fellow warriors. He killed two sailors with his bare hands before Robert Beck, an Irishman, levelled his musket and fired. The ball caught Martin in the chest, and drove him backwards and over the side.

Some say Pierre Martin died that day in 1777. Others say he swam to shore, was cured of his wounds, and fought the British again and again in the years to come.

GAYS RIVER GOLD

Gays River lies midway between Halifax and Truro in Nova Scotia, and in the mid-1800s, it was a gold prospector's paradise.

The digging began in the 1850s, when a tramp found a night's lodging in Dave Corbett's hay barn. The next morning, the tramp went down to the river to wash the sleep from his eyes, and to fill a canteen for the long walk to Halifax. In the running water, he found a fist-sized nugget of gold.

That brought prospectors, speculators, diggers, and panhandlers to Gays River. Gold mines were everywhere. A man named Dan MacDonald claimed he took half a million dollars from one mine, and his success attracted the mining companies. A Boston company bought large tracts of land, built a crusher, and employed a crew of over one hundred men. Then a New York company showed up and bought most of what land was left.

Small-time prospectors leased their diggings from these large companies. Usually, when they struck it rich, the large company let the lease expire and worked the mine itself, thus cutting the prospector out of gaining any profit.

A miner named Moulton wandered into Gays River from Maine, and leased land from the New York company. Moulton was quiet, with a no-nonsense way of going about his business. Sam Mills hired on with Moulton, and to hear Sam tell it, they struck a gold seam in tunnel number one that promised tremendous wealth. But instead of digging straight ahead, Moulton directed Sam and the rest of the crew to dig to the left of the seam. Sure enough, within a few days, the gold played out.

Moulton was no fool. He knew what he had, and did not want the New York company catching on to the rich seam until he had renewed his lease.

Moulton was in New York a few months later, ready to extend his lease with the company, when he suddenly took a heart attack and died.

The New York Company closed the mine after that, believing it to be an empty cavern of mud and granite dust. But in 1960, on good advice, another company opened it up, and found what Moulton had left behind.

A COURTEOUS PRIVATEER

New Englanders and South Shore Nova Scotians regularly engaged in smuggling. They did so openly from port to port, and there were few local officials on either side of the Bay of Fundy who would complain. That is, until 1796, when the British started cracking down on the illegal trade with the Americans.

In June of that year, Captain Richard Perry sailed his American ship, the *Dove of Boston*, into Liverpool harbour. Joshua Newton, the Liverpool justice of the peace—and now an unwilling servant of His Majesty's Customs—declared the cargo contraband, and ordered the sails and spars removed and the ship impounded.

Somewhat embarrassed by the British demand for him to enforce the customs regulations, Joshua Newton took great pains to keep Captain Perry and his crew comfortable and well entertained.

He disagreed with British trade regulations, but was responsible enough to do his best to enforce them.

On June 10, at midnight, Captain Perry and his crew took matters into their own hands. They overtook those guarding the *Dove of Boston* and brought them on board. The crew then broke open the storeroom to get the sails and spars, and within half an hour, the ship had cleared Black's Point outside Liverpool Harbour. There, Captain Perry put the guards ashore with a hearty farewell.

About a week later, Perry sent a courteous letter to Joshua Newton, thanking him for his hospitality and apologizing for the sudden departure of the *Dove of Boston*. Perry explained that he had thought it unnecessary that he be detained any longer. He also begged a pardon for the guards, because they were forced to comply. "I set them ashore," the smuggler wrote, "because they have family, and God forbid, I should be the means of keeping any man from his family."

LAST POST

Fort Anne. December 6, 1739.
Five shadows left him on the floor, shivering at the burning wood and at the silent withering of the night. The darkness choked his courage. The dying firelight seemed to claw its way across the room to scratch at the brass on his blood-soaked tunic, and at his sword, which was unsheathed and stabbed into the floor at his feet.

Lieutenant-Governor Lawrence Armstrong had always known he would one day die by the sword. It is what soldiers do. Yet he had not expected that he would die in a fallen-down fort in Annapolis Royal, Nova Scotia, with five stab wounds in his stomach and breast.

Since serving with the Duke of Marlborough in the Continental Campaign from 1704 to 1709, Armstrong had always imagined himself gored and glorious on a battlefield, face up in the mud, blinking at the sunlight through blue smoke. He had seen himself dying slowly and proudly despite the pain, with his head propped on a soldier's coat and his last words for his regiment.

Those had been his glory days, fighting under the Duke of Marlborough in the War of the Spanish Succession. He remembered the proud march to Oudenaarde, with Belgium women peeking at his column from behind closed shutters, while their men hid on the hillsides and watched the red line of soldiers bend in the sunlight like a willow. And then the battle—which for Armstrong was a skirmish in the lowlands—where a French volley brought him the taste of his own blood.

Those were days only a soldier could have loved: the mud slog and frozen mornings. Bogs weepy with the blood of the dying and the stone-sunk heaviness of the dead. There was a windy bivouac in Flanders, where the night was warmed by a huddle of soldiers breathing memories over a fire. Later, there was a company of officers drunk on brandy—compliments of the Duke of Marlborough himself. After Oudenaarde, there came the battle at Malplaquet, where the Ardennes forest grew stunted and the grass grew thick and tall, and where, for centuries, soldiers had marched to fight and die. The dray carts of the dead had seemed endless on the battlefields and along the corduroy paths. Some said twenty thousand had been killed at Malplaquet. It had been the longest battle of Marlborough's campaign, and Armstrong had proven his courage a dozen times and more. He had proven his willingness to run himself and his regiment against French muzzles and bayonets, and that he was willing to do what soldiers do: die by the sword.

As Armstrong lay on the floor in Fort Anne at Annapolis Royal, blood leaked from his mouth and down his chin. His eyes chased the flames over the floor and wall. Despite the blood in his mouth, he was thirsty for the whiskey that had spilled when the table overturned as he fell. His feet were cold, and his wet fingers were numb from holding back his blood. He rolled his head toward the fire, and groaned to remember the stacks of dead on the battlefields. Twisted legs and arms. Faces bled white despite the brags and promises they had made before the fight. He now regretted that he had missed his own chance to die a soldier's death. His career after Malplaquet had been a great disappointment.

In 1711, Armstrong had served under Sir Hovenden Walker in an expedition to capture Quebec from the St. Lawrence River. The expedition had ended in shipwreck off Île-aux-Oeufs. Nine hundred soldiers and sailors had drowned in the swirling waters, or were battered to death on the underwater ledge. Armstrong's heavy clothes and leather boots had dragged him under and under, where he felt himself rudderless in a dark eternity, drowning—until the sea spit him onto a beach, like a clot unwanted by the froth and spume. He had lost everything to the sea. His money, his personal possessions, his company's arms, munitions, supplies—everything, except what he had been willing to lose: his life.

After that, his tattered company had drawn the short lot to reinforce the garrison at Fort Anne in Annapolis Royal. It was an isolated outpost, which in 1710 had been captured from the French by New England volunteers under Colonel Francis Nicholson. The English had changed the fort's name from Port Royal to Fort Anne, but they had not improved its dilapidated structure.

The following year, the sagged timbers, cracked walls, and rain-scoured earthworks became Armstrong's to command. This was his last post. It was a grumble of discontent with an unfit, unruly garrison. Fort Anne stood as much chance of fighting off a French attack as a sandcastle does at holding back the tide. Yet Armstrong's superiors in Whitehall and Boston had commanded him to defend the fort and guard the land, and to make peace with the Mi'kmaq and the French settlers who called themselves "Acadians."

What the hell did he know about these Acadians, these "ungovernable people" who had refused his solicitations and negotiations as though his words were sharpened on flint and plied into barbs? What did he know about these Popish believers, whose priests had too much to say about everything? What did he know—what does any soldier know—about farmers and farms, except how to run across rows of ploughed land with his bayonet fixed, uncaring for the dead and dying on the thresholds of the barns? And what the hell did he know about this land, except the swamp stink that drifted with mist, and the ice-caked river crushed to the bank of a forest unbroken by sunshine?

He knew little more about commanding a garrison unfit for duty, with soldiers fevered in their bunks, or drunk sick at their posts and in the gutters of the town, piling up grief and grievance along with the piling snow. Armstrong was a soldier—an officer who knew and welcomed the pleasant shiver of running to the battle line, willing himself forward against fear, tightening his ass at the first volley and then pressing on, eager to kill or be killed, to deliver death or receive it. For better or for worse, he had always been a soldier who loved being a soldier. So he prodded the garrison to duty, soldiers and officers alike. He poked commands in their faces, and had some soldiers whipped or made to ride on the sharp spine of a wooden horse when they refused to obey. Which was often. So often that Armstrong stomped around the earthworks and the parade ground with a charged pistol in his belt, and his neck hairs ferreting out the silences for the first signs of mutiny.

At night, he often brooded through the darkness. He sat alone with his whiskey and listened through the lime-plastered walls to his fellow officers, who sat easy in the lamplight, rolling dice and laughing together. He listened for hours, convinced that he heard them plotting to do what they had now finally done.

Armstrong dropped his head into the pooling blood on the floor. His old man's hands slipped from the five stab wounds in his chest and stomach. His eyes rolled back seeing black water and smoke. He listened for his voice calling out, and heard only a millstone busy in the distance.

ENOS COLLINS

Enos Collins was born in Liverpool, Nova Scotia, in 1774, and at an early age, he developed a fondness for money and an eye for opportunity. When he was fifteen years old, he went aboard Nova Scotia privateers, and earned his share of the prize goods captured from French and Spanish merchant ships. By nineteen, he was master of the ship *Adamant*, which sailed the trade triangle between Nova Scotia, the Caribbean, and New England.

When war broke out with the Americans in 1812, Collins was first in line to profit off the fighting. He fitted out several of his own privateers, and made a fortune capturing and selling prize goods off American ships. And when the war ended, Enos Collins turned his privateering business into a more legitimate shipping industry, trading in fish, lumber, coffee, molasses, and rum. He also partnered with Samuel Cunard in the Cunard Shipping Line.

Collins soon had enough capital to start his own bank, the Collins Bank. Not long after, he founded the Halifax Banking Company, the first banking company in Canada, which later morphed into the Canadian Imperial Bank of Commerce.

Collins had a nose for making money, and once he had sniffed out an opportunity, he was quick to act. During the Napoleonic War, he heard that the British Army under Wellington, the Iron Duke, was trapped near Cadiz by the French, and desperate for provisions. Collins fitted out three ships—one from Halifax and two from Saint John—loaded them with food and supplies, sailed the ocean, and ran the French blockade at Cadiz.

Collins did not do so out of a deep love and loyalty for the British Empire. He did it for profit. He keep the provisions on board the ships until Wellington agreed to terms that were favourable to Collins.

Enos Collins was a money-maker, and a no-holds-barred ne-gotiator. By the time he died in 1871, at the age of ninety-seven, he had amassed an estate valued at more than six million dollars. That was a whopping pile of money for the time—so much that he was considered the wealthiest man in North America.

THE ECCENTRIC

He called himself Robert McIntosh, but his right name was Robert Childs. He was born around 1880 in Rexton, Kent County, New Brunswick, and while he was still a young man, he went to Wisconsin, started a business, and made a fortune.

In the early 1900s, Robert Childs returned to New Brunswick, and spent most of his time around Sussex. He often carried thou-sands of dollars in his pockets. Asked why he did this, Childs would shrug and walk off, mumbling about destroying all his money and everything he owned before he died. The few times someone pinned him down to explain this statement, Childs said he'd rather see it all go up in smoke than give anyone else what he had worked so hard to get.

About the middle of May in 1919, Childs bought two revolvers, rented a horse and buggy, and told acquaintances he had land busi-ness to settle at Rexton.

Robert Childs rode up to the family home, the one he had always regarded as his, but which now belonged to his nephew. No one was home. First he set fire to the barn, then he went into the house and kicked burning wood all over the kitchen. He wanted the property destroyed, believing it was his, and not wanting anyone else to have it. But the fires went out before he had reached the nearby woods.

There, he cut brush and piled it around a large pine tree. On this, he stacked all the money he had left—thousands of dollars—and soaked it down with kerosene. Then he climbed the tree and began dropping lighted matches onto the brush below. When he saw one of these catch, he cocked one of the revolvers and shot himself in the face.

Childs came bouncing down through the branches, landed on the brush pile, and snuffed the fire. And that's where the authorities found him—dead on a heap of unburned money.

PREACHERS

In 1850, the Reverend James Porter was pastor of a Saint John, New Brunswick, church. He shook with the spirit when he preached. And he often singled out sinners in his congregation and chastised them from the pulpit for their evil ways and hypocrisy.

Then in 1852, he suddenly resigned his pulpit and the ministry to take a high-paying job as superintendent of schools. After a year or two, he quit that and started his own newspaper, a political sheet called *The Free Press*.

But after about six months, James Porter found the printer's wages not very lucrative, and hired himself out to the Sons of Temperance as a lecturer. He travelled New Brunswick, denouncing the demon drink and crying to one packed lecture hall after another, "Touch not, handle not!"

His preacher's background helped him recognize the true sinners among his audiences: the man who hid a bottle in the barn and nipped while milking or pitching hay, the woman who had a cough every second Sunday, and eased her scratchy throat with sips of brandy. He recognized them and knew them, and singled them out for their weakness.

Then late in 1855, James Porter abandoned the teetotal platform for something more profitable. He applied for and was granted a permit to deal in booze, and as *The Headquarters*, a Fredericton newspaper, reported: "...yesterday's enemy of Demon Rum became the only licensed liquor dealer in the City of Saint John."

James Porter was not the first religion and temperance enthusiast to give himself over to the dark side, nor was he the last.

Reverend R. G. Fulton, a Methodist and a strong temperance advocate, had been pastor of the Centenary Church in Saint John, but in 1927, he had a change of mind. He resigned the ministry and became chairman of the newly formed New Brunswick Liquor Control Commission—the office governing sales of all liquor in the province.

Reverend William B. Tennant was pastor of the Exmouth Street Methodist Church in Saint John, and was also a prohibitionist. But by 1927, Tennant had left the ministry and called himself a "financial agent." Unsociable, and always dressed in funereal black, he travelled about in a chauffeured Pierce-Arrow, worked as bagman (fundraiser) for the Tory Party, and, in the middle of Prohibition, was the managing director of Ready's Brewery.

R. G. Fulton was a somewhat sincere man, W. B. Tennant a thoroughly shady one, and James Porter a flat-out hypocrite.

SERVING THE GREATER GOOD

Every once in a while, good triumphs over evil, and bad men end their lives serving the greater good.

On September 16, 1826, four American sailors arrived in Louisburg aboard a Cape Breton fishing boat. Their names were Charles Merchand, Winslow Curtis, John Hughes, and John Muney. According to Charles Merchand—the one who did all the talking—the sailors had been rescued off a small island after their ship, the brig *Fame*, had sprung a leak on the way to Labrador, and went to the bottom with a load of tobacco, logwood, sugar, and rice.

Merchand never varied his story no matter how many times he told it, which was often—once to the captain of the fishing skiff, twice to the authorities, and again to Mr. Slattery, a local business-man. The sailors had asked Slattery for passage to Halifax on his coastal schooner, in exchange for their help loading his trade goods. From there, Merchand said, they would make their way to Boston.

Merchand, Curtis, and Hughes all had a hard, weathered look to them, like men who had scratched their names on the inside walls of a jail. John Muney was not much more than a boy, and blessed with the soft side of his parents' features. How he came to be with these three toughs was anyone's guess. But Slattery wasn't taking chances. He asked the authorities about the sailors—and that's when he heard the same story repeated almost word for word.

Such unusual consistency peaked Slattery's suspicion. He kept a close eye on the four men, and cocked an ear whenever they huddled in private conversation. Slattery noticed one thing that heightened his distrust: whenever he approached any of the sailors, Merchand seemed to threaten them to silence with a cold, hard stare.

As the men loaded the coaster boat, Slattery managed to gain John Muney's confidence. He took the young man aside, and pressed him on the details of the sailors' leaky ship and island rescue. One question pestered Slattery: what had happened to the captain of the *Fame?* Why hadn't he been rescued with the other men?

Muney went white at the mention of the captain. Then he broke down and confessed what they had done.

They had sailed out of Boston with Captain Edwards, and Thomas Jenkins, the first mate. Merchand had sailed with Captain Edwards before, and held a grudge against him. At night, in the forecastle, he often bragged that one day he would captain his own vessel, and suggested that maybe it would be the one they were now sailing.

Then one night, while Jenkins had the watch, Merchand and Curtis crept from behind and split open Jenkins's head with an axe. Merchand then handed Curtis the axe and ordered him to kill the sleeping captain. But Curtis froze upon entering the captain's quarters, so Merchand grabbed the axe and did it himself.

Muney swore he and Hughes had remained below deck during all the bloodshed. They had known what was going on, he admitted, but did nothing to try and stop it.

"And what about the ship?" Slattery asked.

Muney lowered his head, and confessed that after the murders, Merchand and Curtis had lost their nerve and scuttled the ship to hide what they had done. All four of them had taken turns with the axe, chopping holes in the hull.

Slattery had them arrested and transported to Halifax, where authorities shipped them to Boston for trial. No sooner had the four been thrown into the Boston jail than John Hughes cheated the gallows by opening his wrist with a rusted scrap of iron. The others went to trail for piracy and murder, were found guilty, and were hanged in the jail yard.

As it turned out, these four sailors, who had consorted with evil, ended their earthly existence by serving the greater good. They helped educate a classroom of soon-to-be doctors—as specimens on the dissection table at Harvard Medical School.

CANADIAN SENATE

(BJG)

Among Canadians generally, our Senate is not very popular. Our country has fits of wanting to amend it, or even abolish it completely.

In the Maritimes, individual Senate members are sometimes highly respected, but contempt for the institution itself is no new thing.

William Todd was a highly regarded citizen of St. Stephen, New Brunswick. Here is a letter he wrote to the editor of his local newspaper, the *Saint Croix Courier*:

"Sir, in the Proclamation announcing the Dominion of Canada, I observe my name among those who will be summoned to the Senate. And I beg most respectfully to decline the seat."

The letter is dated June 29, 1867—*before* Confederation. Todd didn't want anything to do with our Senate even before we had one.

New Brunswickers weren't alone in this attitude. Forty-two years after Todd's rejection came this report from the *Saint John Standard*, on December 16, 1909:

Charlottetown, PEI. It is learned that the vacant senatorship was two weeks offered to John McLean, MLA of Souris. Mr. McLean declined the position coupled with the remark that he would rather remain a man than be made a senator.

Senates in North America are counterparts of the House of Lords in Great Britain. In the United States, senators are elected. In Canada, they are appointed, and many people, particularly in the western provinces, are calling for us to adopt the US practice. But before we hurriedly accept the American model maybe we should first look at how the British do it.

Many seats in the House of Lords are inherited, bishops who hold seats are elected to them, other seats are filled by appointment, and still others are simply up for sale to almost anyone who can afford their huge price. A man who grew up on the Miramichi

River, William Max Aiken, bought one of these seats in 1917 and called himself "Lord Beaverbrook." And, in recent years, another newspaper baron, Conrad Black, bought one as well.

Now, if Canada were to start selling its Senate seats for the high price they demand in Great Britain, the revenue gained might go a long way to relieving our national debt.

THE HAYFIELD HAND

Fate is fickle indeed. What it gives in one breath, oftentimes it takes away in another.

In the 1860s, fate brought a young, male stranger to the Musquodoboit Valley in Nova Scotia looking for work. He hammered on Thomas Gladwin's door. Gladwin sized the man up as able enough for hard work and honest-looking enough to hire, and referred him to Mr. Hurley's farm, where Gladwin knew his neighbour needed help with haying.

The man was hired on as a hayfield hand. He bunked in Hurley's barn and took his meals with the family. He said his name was Wilson.

One day he was scything a backfield, when word reached him that Mr. Hurley's daughter had taken ill. Despite the care of a local doctor, her condition grew steadily worse. Wilson inquired after the girl's illness, and upon hearing the details, approached Mr. Hurley and offered to cure his daughter.

Hurley granted permission, and within two days, the girl's health turned for the better.

Now it was Hurley's turn to make inquiries. It turned out the young man's name was Henry Wilson Stone, and that he was a very skilled physician who had run away from England for reasons he would not say. He had gone to Australia first, and then made his way to Nova Scotia, working odd jobs to earn his keep.

Word quickly spread about young Doc Stone. In no time, he had a large medical practice that stretched from Ship Harbour to Gay's River and from Chezzetcook to the Musquodoboits. He eventually married Miss Webber of Lower Lakeville (now Lake Charlotte), and the couple settled on the Wellington Kent farm in Meagher's Grant.

People along the Eastern Shore of Nova Scotia thanked their lucky stars for Doc Stone's fateful arrival. And they made certain Doc and Mrs. Stone knew just how much they were valued. There was always a hamper of dry goods or a tub of salt fish left on the Stones' back porch by way of thank you.

Then one day, in the summer of 1880, Ronald Crawford sent word to the doc that his daughter, Lalia, had taken ill. Doc Stone grabbed his black bag and started out for where the Crawfords lived, near Crawford Falls. But when he reached the bank of the Musquodoboit River, Bill Grant was there waiting. Bill's boy was sick, and he begged Doc Stone to cross the river and look in on his boy before he continued on to the Crawford place.

Doc Stone agreed. Then he stripped naked and tossed his medical bag and clothes into Bill Grant's boat. The doc said the exercise of swimming across the river would do him good and told Bill Grant to follow with his clothes.

Then the doctor entered the water—and that's when fate breathed its second breath over the Musquodoboit Valley. Doc

Stone, the former hayfield hand, swam half a dozen strokes, took a heart attack, and drowned before Bill Grant could reach him.

BILL HEN

Bears once were numerous in New Brunswick and Nova Scotia. And they were a menace to farmers grazing cattle and sheep out beyond the "back forty."

In 1908, when Jonathan Morrison married Bertha Meisner of Meisner Section, Nova Scotia, they set up housekeeping in Springfield, and her father gave them two sheep to start their married life down the road to prosperity. A year later, a bear killed both sheep, and detoured the newlyweds onto a long road of hardship.

Ever since that isolated section of Lunenburg County was settled in 1819, bears have had their way with flocks of sheep. Back then, bears were damn near experts when it came to cleaning up mutton. By the end of the 19th century farmers became desperate. Locals Bob Grinton and Bill Charlton decided to protect their livestock, as well as their neighbours', by trapping as many bears as possible. But for all the bears they trapped, they came up short of the bear-hunting record set at the turn of twentieth century and held by William Henry Merry—known throughout Lunenburg County as "Bill Hen."

When Bill Hen returned from checking his bear traps and deadfalls, people often lined the roadway to see his prize. Bill drove an open-backed wagon with high rear wheels and a high seat. He would stop at one group of onlookers after another, and let them gander at the dead bear crammed inside with its pig-eyed head propped on the rim of the wagon. People always pestered him with questions about the hunt, but Bill Hen seldom answered. Bill was not a talker, and he chewed more words than he spoke. He rarely shared his stories of risking life and limb hunting bears.

However, on one occasion, he did.

It was the winter of 1904 or 1905, and Bill was snowshoeing across country with a brace of snared rabbits dangling from his backpack. He hit a patch of crusted snow that suddenly caved and dropped him headlong into an immense drift, close to an uprooted tree. As he struggled to free himself, Bill discovered he had company in that snow-drifted hollow: two sleeping bears.

Luckily, Bill still had his rifle, and now, as the two bears tried to focus their sleepy eyes on the intruder, Bill shot them both. He later said he couldn't afford not to kill them. After all, Bill made his living hunting bears, and winter was a lean time for bagging one. Besides, in those years a good bearskin was worth twenty dollars, and they were in high demand as sleigh robes, rugs, stoles, and muffs.

Sheep farmers praised Bill as their benefactor, and rural communities as their protector. They considered William Henry Merry the best bear hunter of all time. Most could only guess at the number of bears Bill had killed in Lunenburg County. But those who knew Bill well enough to drop in for a visit only had to tally the 127 notches on his doorjamb to know just how good a bear hunter he was.

DAVID POWER

The Power family—made up of a husband, a wife, and seven children—arrived in Prince Edward Island rolled up tight in a threadbare wrapper of poverty. Their lives in Ireland had consisted of one miserable circumstance piled upon another. But now, with their feet planted on a plot of land in Prince County as tenant farmers, and with their field planted and their half-grown pig plumping up for slaughter, they saw hope sparkling in the morning sun.

David, the father, brimmed with expectation. He was honest, sober, and willing to work the pads off his hands to make the most of this opportunity to improve his lot in life. But hard work and hope-filled dreams are sometimes not enough to keep clouds from dulling the sunlight. Come fall, the crop yielded less than anticipated, but enough, according to his wife's reckoning, to scrape by for another year—barely.

So on a November morning in 1827, after heaving a month-long sigh of disappointment, David's Celtic fury darkened into his red hair when he heard his pig squeal in distress and saw a bear carrying it from the pen.

David Power did not own a gun, but he did lay claim to a heart swollen with courage and determination. He rushed into the cabin and hauled a tightly woven rug from the floor—a family treasure his wife had carted from their hovel in Ireland. Then he ordered his oldest son, Patrick, to grab a club and follow.

The bear had made straight for the forest with the porker in its grasp, but a rail fence proved too much for it to scale without letting go of the squealing pig. The bear held on and pushed against the fence, then struggled to squeeze through.

After running across the field lugging that heavy carpet, David was darn near exhausted when he and his son reached the angry bear. He draped the carpet over the bear and the pig and held on with all the might he had left.

Patrick, a strapping lad himself, let loose a wallop that stunned the bear enough for the pig to get free. Then he rained furious blows on the carpeted bear. By the time the bear sagged lifeless under that carpet, two neighbours had raced over to investigate the commotion. David's wife and family had hurried across the field as well.

According to the newspaper account: "After a due amount of rejoicing and congratulations, there was a triumphal procession, the central figures being David, Patrick, and the lifeless thief."

As it turned out, beating that bear to death not only saved their pig for next year's slaughter, but also returned their family spirit to one of hope and great expectation. It seems the government offered a bounty of ten shillings for the nose of a bear. That reward went a long way toward seeing David and his family through the long PEI winter and the blossoming spring, and on into a bumper crop that fall, with two pigs in the pen and a cow in the barn.

AFTER-DINNER CONVERSATION

It is written in 1 Kings 18:27, "the devil is either talking or pursuing." On July 20, 1820, the Nova Scotia Supreme Court ruled Major George Barrow had been doing both.

In 1820, in Halifax, William Henry Hall fell on hard times and incurred more debt than he was able to secure with what little property he owned. He was also cash-strapped, and could not meet the payment terms on his loans.

His creditors forced the issue, and had William Hall locked away in jail until he could pay what he owed. How a debtor who could not raise sufficient cash on the outside was expected to do so behind bars is a conundrum that challenged legal minds even then. Unless they were visited by a guardian angel, debtors stood a good chance of spending the rest of their lives in jail. That was the prospect facing William Hall—and Major George Barrow hoped for nothing less.

No sooner had William Hall entered the jailhouse than Major Barrow started making regular visits to Hall's wife. According to court documents, Barrow got the woman drunk a number of times, and stayed late into the night.

Hall's wife was not an innocent, and was easily seduced by the charms of Major Barrow. On numerous occasions, while her husband was in jail, she sneaked about town for clandestine meetings with the major, and once she did so in disguise.

When word reached the jailhouse and Hall heard about his wife's behaviour, he sued Major Barrow on the grounds of "engaging in criminal conversation with the plaintiff's wife."

After hearing all the sordid details of the affair, the Supreme Court ruled in Hall's favour, and awarded him damages of five hundred pounds.

It just so happened that the amount of the settlement covered

William Hall's debts. Upon his release, Hall's wife fell into his arms, sobbing mightily and gushing with promises of her true love.

One wonders if Hall's wife was a lonely, love-starved victim to Major Barrow's affections, or if she was Hall's guardian angel, coming onto Major Barrow while wrapped in the red cloak of the devil, both talking and pursuing. After all, William's award of five hundred pounds and his release from debtor's prison had turned on her frequent after-dinner conversations with the major.

BEN WORTH

When the Americans revolted against Great Britain in 1776, Ben Worth declared himself for the British. He wanted nothing to do with revolution and the aggravation it brought to hard-working, peace-minded men and women. And he wanted less to do with the American Sons of Liberty, who were not much better than thugs and bullyboys, given the way they persecuted those who did not join their side.

Ben was a Loyalist, but not the stay-at-home kind who lived a soft life under the protection of the British Army. Ben Worth risked his body and bones for what he believed, and for the 150 acres he owned on the New Jersey side of the Hudson River: he became a spy for the British general William Howe, and sneaked back and forth across the river to record the troop movements of George Washington's army on the New York side.

In 1777, Ben was on a bluff overlooking Washington's encampment on Harlem Heights, and counting campfires to tally the number of enemy soldiers. He got so engrossed in keeping count that he failed to hear a rebel patrol creeping up from behind. All at once, the rebels pounced and took Ben prisoner.

Washington charged Ben with spying and tried him before a military tribunal. The tribunal found Ben guilty, and had his right thumb branded with the letter *T* for traitor. Ben was lucky: convicted spies usually went before a firing squad. Less than a year before, General William Howe had ordered the execution of Nathan Hale, a Connecticut schoolmaster, for spying on Washington's behalf. Washington's military tribunal could just as easily have sentenced Ben Worth to the same.

After the Revolution, Ben made his way to Halifax. In 1786, he went on to Cape Breton, where he settled first in Glengarry (now West Mabou), and later at Mill River. Folks in Glengarry and Mill River admired this man of courage. They also valued his ingenuity. Ben knew all about machinery, especially water wheels. He had built them in New Jersey, and now he built them in Cape Breton.

Ben Worth's water wheels powered gristmills, sawmills, and even the machinery in small factories. His skill and ingenuity helped turn pioneer settlements in Cape Breton into thriving communities.

He died in 1827, and the only monument to his life is a slate headstone in the Pioneer Cemetery on the Rankinville Road. The cemetery sits on a cliff overlooking the Mabou River, and the inscription on the headstone reads: "Here lies Benjamin Worth, one of the first settlers of Mabou—came from New Jersey in 1786."

MATHIAS'S DREAM

(BJG)

Mathias Roussell of Edmundston, New Brunswick, put a lot of stock in the truth of dreams, and as it turned out, it was a good thing he did.

Mathias had worked the winter of 1928 to 1929 in a lumber camp in northern New Brunswick. On his way home, he lost $225 in cash—his whole season's earnings. That was a lot of money in 1929, money the thirty-three-year-old needed to pay the bills his wife and children had run up while he was away.

People said the loss of the money unhinged Roussell's mind—at least for a time—because on August 12, he told his family he was going to look for woods work on the Allagash River in Maine. Only he went in a different direction: he headed for the upper reaches of Green River, New Brunswick, then a perfect wilderness.

Mathias took little with him—not even a jackknife—and left with only the summer clothing on his back. He walked for weeks, walking the soles off his boots and turning his clothes to rags. He survived on berries until the October cold killed them off. Then he turned to eating nuts, roots, and tree cones.

Later, he told how there came a night when cold, hunger, and exhaustion struck so hard that he lay down expecting never to get up again. He fell into a kind of sleep, and in that sleep came a dream. In the dream, Mathias saw his long-dead mother. She was calling for him to come back home, and she even showed him the way, for he was hopelessly lost.

On waking, Mathias recalled the dream with perfect clarity—even the directions his mother had given him—and somehow that gave him hope and new strength. He followed his mother's directions, but it wasn't easy. He had to ford a stream up to his neck in icy water, and he met a bear face to face, but both he and the bear were so surprised, they ran in opposite directions.

Then he happened onto a vacant lumber camp, where he found a discarded pair of boots. That made walking a whole lot easier, and within a few more days of bushwhacking through the New Brunswick forest, he broke out into civilization—not near his Edmundston home, but in St. Joseph Parish. He was in what the local newspaper called "a pitiable condition." Still in shock from his frightful experience, he was at first afraid to talk to anyone or approach anyone's house.

But Mathias Roussell would be all right, because his dream had led him to a farm shed whose owner found Mathias asleep on a pile of straw. The owner was Edmond Bosse—Mathias's cousin.

MIRACLE DRUGS

With all the pharmaceutical drugs we have at hand, and with some of the exaggerated claims of natural medicines, you would think most of us would outlive Methuselah. We pretty much have a drug for most of what ails us. And whatever one drug can't cure, another can dope us so dizzy we don't feel the pain.

But this is not new, and certainly not the result of modern science. Today's miracle drugs have nothing over the accomplishments of ointments, elixirs, and decoctions from days gone by.

In 1775, when Simeon Perkins of Liverpool, Nova Scotia, caught the flu, he headed straight for the butter churn. There was nothing like newly churned butter with the curd skimmed off to chase the flu bug from a body; two spoonfuls taken two or three times per day was all it took. At night he'd rub goose oil on the soles of his feet and goose grease on his chest.

And if that didn't rid his body of ailments from the flu, he would then spend an hour the next day hopping back and forth across a narrow stream of water. There was noting like crossing water to cure the flu.

Reverend Mather Byles was an Anglican minister in Saint John in the 1790s. He suffered unmercifully from rheumatism, and from lumbago—severe pain in his lower back. To keep his joints loose and his back pain-free, he faithfully carried a nephrite stone in his hip pocket. This was a piece of jade, and Reverend Byles swore by its medicinal properties—so much so that his son-in-law in Halifax, Doctor Almon, carried one of his own.

Dr. Almon may not have been the most dependable witness for proving the medical effectiveness of a piece of jade. He was the same Dr. Almon who treated his wife for a liver ailment for nearly ten years. She died in July 1787 from what he had diagnosed as an ulcerated liver.

However, before her death, she insisted that her husband perform an autopsy on her body, for the sake of others who might one day suffer from the same ailment. Dr. Almon did as his wife had requested. He discovered that her liver had been normal. The cause of death was "totally owing to the pernicious practice of lacing and girding her corset too tight."

Later, when the good doctor was asked if he had a remedy that would relieve a woman from suffering what his wife had suffered, Almon simply replied, "a healthy dose of common sense."

Fancy concoctions never lost their superstitious attraction in the early Maritimes. They got more and more sophisticated, but no less strange.

James F. Gale, a druggist in Fredericton, ran this ad in the local newspaper in 1845:

"When Algiers fell into the hands of the French, General de Lormont visited the dungeons to liberate the prisoners and what to his astonishment to find two beautiful Spanish girls, pale with grief. But it was not long before they overcame the ravages of confinement, and then only by Holloway's Ointment and Holloway's Pills. Recommended in all disorders, such as Cancer, paralysis, sore nipples, Piles and the bite of mosquitoes…"

Two years later, George Garrity's Botanical Dispensary in Oromocto advertised 112 cure-alls guaranteed to cover sixty-five different ailments. Among the nostrums were: "worm syrup, female strengthening syrup, elixir of life, and skunk Cabbage." And the treatable troubles included: "Lock jaw, gangrene, leprosy and female complaints."

In 1886, Charles Moffitt, a carpenter in Fredericton, recorded in his diary that he "felt bad with a looseness of bowels. Mr. Alexander made me a dose of brandy, laudanum and ammonia which relieved me very much."

Most know what brandy and ammonia are, and laudanum is opium dissolved in alcohol. Even if the mixture didn't cure Moffitt's ills, it certainly took his mind off them.

EARLY DAYS

AND

EVERY DAYS

BOOZE

Between Thursday night and Sunday morning, the downtown Halifax bars are crowded to overflowing. Drunken men and women pour onto the streets, staggering to the next watering hole or stumbling their way home. Haligonians come by their excessive thirst for alcohol honestly—they descend from a long line of beer heads and rum sots.

From the first days of settlement in Halifax, booze had its priority. The first public building erected in Halifax was the king's brewery. Grog shops and taverns came next. They lined the muddy, cart-rutted streets, and both raggedy and finely dressed customers spilled from their doors at all hours of the day and night. The customers staggered from shop to tavern, some unruly and others insensibly drunk. These were the days when a full bowl of bumbo, a concoction of rum, sugar, water, and nutmeg began and ended everyone's workday, from the scullery maid to the governor himself. Rum and beer were even on the daily menu at the Halifax Orphanage, and it was not until 1754 that these items were replaced with spruce beer.

When the brig *Ann* anchored in Halifax Harbour in 1750, townsfolk offered the German settlers jobs in the public works at a wage of two shillings per day, plus a supply of beer and rum. Truckers and labourers, carpenters and boot makers, judges, magistrates, and political leaders all needed a stimulating bowl of rum before starting work in the morning. Among British officers, it was common for those of the higher ranks to start the workday with what they called a "morner" or an "anti-fogmatic": a jolt of rum to clear their heads of the excesses of the night before.

At noon, it was more of the same, and at night it was more again—much more. Soldiers and citizens drank to raise hell one day, and to chase the devil's illness from their bodies the next. As G. Townshend of Halifax wrote to Ward Chipman of Saint John: "My friend Mr. McG here will give you both hogsheads of some old Madeira to keep the gout from your stomach…"

It was said that James Monk—a judge in the Halifax Court of Common Pleas during the 1750s—could "dispose of six bottles of claret at a sitting better than he could settle knotty questions of law." Monk must have eaten enormously while he drank, because he was so obese that no vehicle in Halifax could carry him. He became a laughingstock, and the measure for hugeness in early Halifax. "How big was it?" someone would ask. And the other would answer: "As big as James Monk!"

In 1759, Governor Charles Lawrence removed Monk from the bench "for non-attendance." Clearly, the bottle or a leg of lamb had come between the judge and his duties.

Alexander Grant, a member of the Executive Council—the governing body of the day in Halifax—wrote Reverend Ezra Stiles in May 1760: "…the business of one-half the town is to sell rum, and of the other half to drink it. You may from this single circumstance, judge of our morals, and naturally infer that we are not enthusiastic in religion."

Governor Edward Cornwallis knew the value that early settlers placed on rum. On April 30, 1750, he wrote the Lords of Trade in England, and explained that if he failed to keep public money circulating, town lots "would be given for a gallon of rum."

In the same dispatch, Governor Edward Cornwallis reported that Mr. Townshend supplied 2,500 Halifax settlers with 20,300 gallons of rum—for one year. And that doesn't count copious amounts of beer, wine, and gin also washing through the town. A 1756 census revealed that between 1750 and 1755, this same number of Haligonians, along with a military garrison of approximately three thousand soldiers, consumed an average of seventy to one hundred thousand gallons of liquor per year. And that's what was legally entering Nova Scotia. One can only guess at the quantity of booze smuggled into the province.

Even the gentry had a hand in smuggling quantities of "oh-be-joyful" into Nova Scotia. In a letter dated March 29, 1821, William Griffith advised Sir Brenton Halliburton that he was shipping several bottles of claret and white wine from Bermuda. If Halliburton liked the wine, Griffith offered him a share in a cask of claret, adding: "Say nothing about it to anybody, for fear we should have the Revenue people interfering."

The census numbers for liquor consumption do not account for privately owned stills in Halifax. In 1753, William Best, a master mason, and John Clewly, a master carpenter, inspected the safety of the stills in Halifax. They declared Richard Bower's two stills on Granville Street, and Jonathan Gifford's still on Barrington Street, were safe and well-constructed. But William Murray's still on Grafton Street was a fire hazard. (At this time, stills consisted of open fires under large, sealed cauldrons.)

By 1758, the increased number of people boiling mash threatened Halifax—a town made up of wood-framed buildings—with a serious conflagration. For this reason, the House of Assembly banned stills within the town, or within a quarter-mile of its picket lines. Violators received a fine of one hundred pounds. Joshua Mauger and Joseph Prescott grudgingly suffered the expense of moving their cranes, cauldrons, and molasses barrels outside the picket lines. They complained bitterly to the Executive Council.

Along Barrack Street (now Brunswick Street) in the upper part of town, and near the dockyard on Water Street, there were other places where a thirsty man or woman could buy a drink. In these haunts, a soldier or labourer could wager a week's pay on the turn of a card, or satisfy their lust with a flaxen-haired whore. These were the dirty, single-story houses where no official-looking sign advertised "Spirituous Liquors Sold here by Licence." No, indeed. The proprietors of these grog shops held no liquor licences. These were the outlaw liquor dealers.

In 1750, the Executive Council estimated there were more than forty outlaw liquor dealers in town. It declared that a "corporal punishment ought to be inflicted such as would render the Retailers infamous." Anyone caught selling liquor without a licence sat one hour in the stocks for the first offence, and received twenty stripes on their bare back for a second. In the first few days of that year, the lineup at the whipping post included Mary Eunice, Michael Mounen, John Calahand, and Sarah Dale.

The whipping post must have taught Mary Eunice and Sarah Dale nothing, because the following year, they were back again on the same charge. This time, the court fined them ten pounds and added another thirty stripes to the criss-cross patterns on their bare backs.

Taking their turn at the whipping post for selling liquor without a license were Benjamin Stoner, John Petty, and James Follin. Another unlicensed dealer was also nabbed, a man named Kenner. The court fined him ten pounds. Then, in an unusual discharge of justice, the bailiff gave him back five pounds—because he had turned Crown witness and informed on himself.

Over the years, the outlaw dealers learned to add value to their liquor sales. Besides selling booze, John Clary kept a "disorderly house," in other words a brothel. Henry Carter faced an indictment in March 1792 for having a disorderly house that was "pregnant with evil." Robert Grant sold booze and women from his whorehouse on Barrack Street, and Ann Burroughs gave him competition nearby. Jane Mayberry sold liquor and her personal services from her room in Thomas Cleve's house, and Eleanor Porter entertained the men of the town wherever and whenever she could. Ann Jeffs and Margaret Arthur were partners in a disorderly house that entertained "evil men and women during all hours of the night with drinking, tippling, whoring, and misbehaving themselves."

Rum revenue financed the government. It paid for judges, constables, and clerks. It built public highways and wharves, and provisioned the workhouse, the poorhouse, and the town hospital. To ensure that this invaluable source of revenue continued, Governor Charles Lawrence issued a general warrant authorizing John Woodin to "search all warehouses and inspect all goods landed to secure the duties on Rum and other Spirituous Liquors."

Woodin also had the authority to stop anyone on the streets and roads to search them for liquor, and he could enter any home or business he might suspect of selling booze. For his efforts, John Woodin received half the value of all the goods he seized. Needless to say, Woodin exercised his authority with great enthusiasm.

Of course, all this drinking had its social consequences. Rum might have warmed the settlers' blood during that first winter in 1749, but it also soaked their enthusiasm for work the following spring. Drunkenness left them listless and unproductive, and many were incapable of meeting the rugged demands of a frontier settlement.

Governor Charles Lawrence bemoaned the degenerate effect that excessive drinking had on the population: "I really wish too great a latitude may not be indulged to the continuance and increase of that most pernicious commerce of importing and retailing Spirituous Liquors, which has been so much the Bane of Industry, as well as the health of the people here, and which the governors have been struggling against from the commencement of the settlement."

And this from the grand jury: "...it is not uncommon to meet, at all times of the day, people staggering in the streets, oppressed with intoxication; while others, in a still worse condition, are found lying in a manner disgraceful to the police of any civilized country; and, however, shocking it may be to Humanity, the Grand Jury declare, that to their knowledge many persons have died in the streets, whose deaths were attributed solely to excessive drinking."

Alexander Andrews spent April 23, 1752, drinking with friends. That night, he staggered into Captain Cook's grog shop and dropped dead from drink. Similarly, Widow Lush lived true to her name. She kept a tavern in town, and on December 18, 1753, after a night of partying, she took a fit outside her front door and died. The coroner ruled: "died by intoxication."

Twenty-seven years later, the grand jury reported no change in popular habit: "…the lower sort of people in the Town of Halifax and its Vicinity are addicted in the most shameful manner to the vice of drunkenness." The following year, Mather Byles wrote to his sisters in Boston: "Rheumatisms and Rum-ma-tisms are the two endemical diseases of Halifax."

If "rum-ma-tism" was indeed a disease, then John Kervin had it bad. In February 1827, he and three friends were on Cunard's Wharf drinking from a puncheon of rum. (A puncheon was a large cask that held between seventy and one hundred gallons.) They took turns with a stalk of kelp, using it to suck rum from the bunghole. Kervin drank and drank to his heart's content; then he and a companion staggered from the wharf and headed down Water Street, where they entered a house. Both immediately passed out. Kervin's companion woke a few hours later—but Kervin didn't. A coroner examined Kervin's body, and ruled that he died "from excessive liquor."

On December 30, 1832, Thomas Harris also died from intoxication—and he was in jail. Fellow prisoners reported Harris as constantly drunk, and John Fielding, the jailer, testified to the coroner's jury that Harris "was drunk that day, but because he was generally that way, I took no notice of it."

In 1834, Mary Walsh died horribly from heavy drinking. She and Bridgett Sullivan had spent three days drunk in their rented room at Robert Thompson's house. On the night of November 5, they sat on chairs before a roaring fire, drinking and napping. As Mary Walsh drifted into a drunken sleep, she slipped from her chair and into the fire. Robert Thompson smelled the burning flesh, and rushed into the room. Too late! He found Bridgett Sullivan still fast asleep in her chair. At her feet was Mary Walsh's charred corpse.

As people guzzled, they lost their inhibitions and became rowdy, belligerent, and often very violent. On the night of April 1, 1754, while returning to the barracks from a drinking party, a soldier smashed his elbow through the glass window of a private dwelling. The enraged and drunken householder staggered into the street with a cutlass in his hand. He stabbed the soldier twice, then chopped through a new pair of double-channel pumps and separated the soldier from three of his toes.

Drunkenness was John Brisbane's only excuse for assaulting David Ogilvy with the intent to commit sodomy. Moreover, Alexander McManus, Robert Sarty, and William Coffee offered drunkenness as an excuse for raping and murdering Mary Penfold, who was a thief and prostitute.

Drunkenness also led to innumerable non-violent crimes. Ann Allen stole for the sake of drink. In 1759, she took a shirt from Enoc Wiswell and sold it to Margaret Conway for a gallon of rum. Henry Fuller complained to the Court of General Quarter Sessions that his wife, Mary, was constantly drunk from cockcrow to curfew, and had recently stolen his watch to procure money for drink.

Other thieves, such as Alice Wallace, preyed on those who could not hold their liquor. She filched a watch from John Fuller's pocket as he sat in the street in a drunken stupor. Still others shamed themselves and their families after a night of drunken perversion.

James Ramsey, a magistrate, caught John Smith and Prince, a black servant, "in the act of copulation" behind the fence at Lowe's field. Both men received thirty-nine lashes, but Prince also had to suffer the embarrassment of parading through the streets at midday with a sign on his chest announcing his shame to the public.

In the hellholes on Barrack Street, such as Murphy's Waterloo Tavern and the Seven Steps to Hell, and in the dimly lit, undecorated drinking houses (licensed and unlicensed) on the waterfront, men and women brawled, whored, drank, and plotted robbery and murder. In 1787, the grand jury reported "that the disorders which have occasioned the number of indictments laid before the Grand Jury have originated generally in the houses licensed to keep taverns, and in others selling spirituous liquor."

The upper crust enjoyed long bouts of drunkenness as well. William Dyott described a Saint Patrick's Day dinner in 1787 that included the bright lights of Halifax society. "We kept the day in honour of St. Patrick by dining together at the coffee-house, and a pretty scene of drunkenness it was. I stayed in town till the 25th (March), leading a life of debauchery."

A few months later, Prince William Henry and Governor John Wentworth joined twenty members of the Society of the Blue and Orange for a party on November 9. They drank sixty-three bottles of wine and toasted twenty-six bumpers without halt. Dyott claimed that he "never saw such fair drinking."

In the eighteenth century, Halifax was a brawling, drunken seaport, a place where rum was king, and the populace—from a butcher's apprentice on the Market Wharf to a swaggering captain of the night watch, and even the governor himself—paid homage appropriately. The government taxed the rum, the merchants sold it, and everyone drank it. Streets swirled, egos swelled, and livers shrivelled.

In the past three centuries, Halifax has gone from a settlement of wood-framed houses to a big city of concrete and glass. However, a weekend stroll along downtown streets during the small hours of the morning will reveal that when it comes to boozing and brawling, not a whole lot has changed.

RAILWAY TRAGEDY

In early May 1920, an all-night downpour weakened about one hundred yards of the rail line that ran north from Marysville, New Brunswick. A man standing on the south bank of the Nashwaak River stared in horror at what was about to happen. He was brother to the engineer of an approaching train, and there was nothing he could do but watch as the train hit the weak spot.

As the ground gave way, there was an instant when the train almost seemed suspended in mid-air. Then the locomotive and the tender plunged into about twelve feet of water.

The engineer, John Gillies of Newcastle, died instantly, but his cab companion, fireman John Estabrooks of Fredericton, was not so lucky. When the train fell, the steel plates that formed the floors of the engine and the tender separated for a moment. Then they closed again, pinning one of Estabrooks's legs between them, and leaving him standing in agony in about five feet of water. Finally, the massive machine began to settle—ever so slowly—into the soft mud of the Nashwaak.

The man on the south bank continued to stare at the tragedy unfolding before him, and he later reported all that he saw to the *Daily Gleaner* newspaper in Fredericton.

Railway officials called for a crane, but they knew by the way the engine continued to settle into the soft mud that help would not make it in time. Other railway workers summoned doctors from Fredericton, but they didn't arrive until the water was well past Estabrooks's neck.

Time and again, Estabrooks begged the surgeons to reach beneath the water and cut off his leg. They refused. Their only offering was a long pull on a bottle of whiskey.

Estabrooks writhed in agony for another hour, as the engine slowly settled. Then, at about 5:10 that afternoon, the water finally reached his mouth. As dozens stood on the riverbank and watched, John Estabrooks drowned.

THE SCOTT ACT

The Scott Act passed through Parliament in 1878, granting municipalities the option to prohibit the sale of liquor within their jurisdictions. Fredericton, the capital of New Brunswick, was the first town in the Dominion to adopt the Scott Act—and the last to observe it. Many other Maritime municipalities followed Fredericton's lead.

In the forty-odd years that the Scott Act was on the books, no one in Fredericton—or in any part of Eastern Canada, for that matter—had to go for long without a drink.

In one Fredericton hotel in the early 1880s, anyone inquiring was told straight-out that the establishment did not sell liquor. But even as the clerk spoke those words, he was winking, and motioning to a backroom.

To obtain a bootlegging conviction, a complainant had to identify the seller. This was easier said than done in that Fredericton hotel. In the backroom, the person passing out the booze was gowned top-to-bottom in a white sheet, and his face hidden by a black mask. Few knew who their server was, and those who did weren't telling.

A rum dealer in Crapaud, Prince Edward Island, was even more ingenious at hiding his identity. He had a turntable built into a wall. The money went in, and a bottle came out.

In a better class of Fredericton hotel—one down on the riverfront—backroom regulars served themselves from shelves of booze and a supply of tumblers. Near the door stood a small box with a slot in the top. The box bore a sign saying "Diocesan Society." The regulars were always charitable in proportion to what they consumed.

LANDING ON YOUR FEET

When Captain Lowden sailed into Pictou Harbour in 1779, he had blood in his eyes and just one thing on his mind: vengeance. A handful of coastal pirates near Pictou had raided his ship, robbed the cargo, and locked him in the hold. Lowden had escaped in the nick of time to steer the ship from running aground, and now he was hard after the criminals.

But Captain Lowden was dumb out of luck, because the residents of Pictou had helped the coastal raiders escape the county. Captain Lowden was not a very likable man. He was a toughened sea captain who had once been employed in the unsavoury business of transporting convicts to Virginia and Bermuda. The Pictou settlers preferred helping the coastal raiders to the likes of Captain Lowden.

Nevertheless, the captain had a legal grievance that demanded compensation, and the local magistrate, Robert Patterson, was obliged to settle it. Magistrate Patterson could not ask Pictou residents to cough up the money to compensate the captain—not without jeopardizing his own peace and tranquillity. What Patterson needed was a means of raising the money without offending his fellow Pictonians.

His eyes fell on Wellwood Waugh, a strict Scottish Presbyterian, who in previous years had refused to swear an oath of allegiance to the British Crown because it violated his religious principles. Blaming Wellwood Waugh for helping the coastal raiders, whether he had or not, would upset no one in Pictou besides Waugh himself.

Patterson ordered that Waugh's property and possessions be seized and sold at public auction, with the proceeds used to compensate Captain Lowden. Patterson then ordered Wellwood Waugh to clear out of town. And that settled things to everyone's satisfaction—including Wellwood Waugh's, though he did not know it at the time.

Waugh left Pictou, and squatted on a piece of ground near Tatamagouche. There he got into the shipbuilding business and made himself a fortune. The place where he settled became known as Waugh's River.

DRIVING ON THE RIGHT

When we slip behind the wheel of a car, we do so on the left-hand side. Then we drive on the right-hand side of the road. In the Maritimes, this was not always so.

If a horse is pulling a buggy, it doesn't like being driven from the left. Therefore, its driver sits on the right-hand side of the seat. When Britain built its first motorcars, these imitated buggies, and British automakers put the steering wheel—and thus the driver— on the right-hand side. When meeting another vehicle, it's safer for a driver to be on the same side of the car as an oncoming driver, so the British drove on the left side of the road.

United States automakers didn't consider the horse, but the human, and because most of us are right-handed, they put the driver on the left, leaving his right hand free to shift gears. With the driver on the left, US government regulation forced automobiles to travel on the right side of the road, for safety's sake.

Confusing? It gets worse!

Maritimers followed British regulations, with the driver sitting on the right side of the car and driving on the left side of the road. But because most of our vehicles were made in the US, driving in the left lane was dangerous. And when either a Maritimer or an American crossed the border, results could be disastrous.

For example, in October 1922, Harry Bell—an alderman from Woodstock, New Brunswick was driving in Centreville, New Brunswick, when a sharp turn brought him radiator-to-radiator with an American car driving full bore in Bell's lane. Harry Bell swung his steering wheel and swerved his vehicle into a ditch, nearly killing himself in the process.

Thirty minutes later, he was on the telephone to his good friend the premier, telling him that he just had to change things.

The changeover came to the Maritimes that same year: on December 1, 1922. Maritimers had to seal up streetcar doors and cut new ones on the opposite side to accommodate. They also had to get used to driving on the right and staying on the right. There were some panic situations, but all in all, Maritimers made the change well enough. And today we just wonder at the British driving on the wrong side of the road.

ASYLUM

The cornerstone of the New Brunswick asylum for the insane, then called the Provincial Lunatic Asylum, was laid in Saint John in June 1847. Present at the ceremony were many dignitaries and special guests, making it a gala outing.

A local newspaper said: "We could not help expressing a secret wish that the Asylum might stand more as a monument to the benevolence of the people, than for any real use."

The ceremonies ended with a dinner at one of the town's leading hotels, befitting a day of civic pride.

Thirteen years later, the pride was still there, evidenced in a Woodstock newspaperman's glowing account of a visit to the place.

The asylum was perched atop a hill at what was then called Fairville, and it commanded a view of the Reversing Falls. The "beauty" (as he called it) enthralled the reporter. "The views from many of the upper windows are beautiful beyond description. Though the air, smoked filled, prevented our seeing any distance."

But it was the asylum's interior that left indelible impressions on the writer. There, he found what he called "perfect order, cleanliness, and quiet," and even among the most dangerous inmates, there was, he said, "no violence or impropriety of language or gesture."

Many patients he found outside, *"assisting voluntarily of course"* in farm work and gardening, and others he found inside, doing appropriate chores.

The asylum's director, Dr. Waddell, explained that in the patients' work, "The superfluous steam is got rid of, and the minds are thus abstracted from baneful excitement, thus health of body and mind is promoted."

The doctor closed with an afterthought on all this. Said he: "Because the inmates perform so much work, the expenses of the Asylum are much reduced."

In early Halifax, the local jail housed criminals in the same cells as the poor, insane, and orphaned. By the early nineteenth century, orphans had their own accommodations, but the poor and the insane still shared their bunks with criminals. The conditions were horrifying: disease-ridden and vermin-infested. Sickness was rampant.

In March 1832, the Halifax grand jury thought of a way to improve the unhealthy conditions of the jail. It recommended granting the faculty at the medical school and their students permission to "participate in the advantages of the Asylum provided they perform a portion of the duties, thus alleviating the workload of the attendants. The sick would thus be better treated and at much less cost."

Their intention was not entirely benevolent toward the poor and the insane. The grand jury added that the asylum "should be so laid open as to make it a useful Medical School, towards which the funds of each student admitted should pay a small annual fee."

In other words, medical students, for a fee, would have a crop of live bodies to practice on.

WHAT'S IN A NAME?

The St. Croix River helps separate New Brunswick from the state of Maine, and there's a small island in its estuary where explorers Pierre du Gua, sieur de Monts, and Samuel de Champlain supposedly spent the winter of 1604. It is further supposed that they named the island "Ile de St. Croix."

The town of St. Stephen, New Brunswick, is on the bank of the St. Croix River. In 1867, its newspaper did not dispute the island's French name, but said it was later called "Neutral Island" because neither Britain nor the United States claimed it. The same paper added that the island had also been called "Doucet Island," which got mangled into many forms, including "Dotler, Dosher, Dotius, and Docic."

Edward Jack, an employee of the Crown Land Office and a respected antiquarian, wrote that in 1797 the island was renamed "Bone Island"—probably an English corruption of the French "Bon-Ile," or "Good Island." Jack goes on to explain that "Dotius" and its related variations arose when a group of men visited the island in the early 1800s, and one of them named it "Dosia's Island" after a girlfriend, Theodosia Millberry.

On today's map, it appears as "Dochet Island," and most people pronounce it "doe-shay."

Historians believe that the island is much smaller today than it was in 1604—it has been eroded by strong tides and currents, and rising sea levels. But maybe, just maybe, that island in the St. Croix River is worn down and sinking from the sheer weight of so many names.

FIRE

On November 6, 1882, at 11:50 P.M., most of the 343 inmates of the poor asylum in Halifax were asleep when a fire broke out in the bakeshop of the building's Victorian structure. The fire burned slowly across the ground floor, until it reached the elevator shaft. Then, on the updraft of air, the fire roared to the upper floors and filled them with flames.

The dry timbers, floor planks, and wall boards burned like tinder. Within minutes, the entire building screamed with the blaze, which was soon burning so hot that iron nails turned bright blue and exploded like gunshots. Lead roof seams melted and dripped in liquid flames over the eaves. Large, slate roofing shingles cracked free and slid from the angular roof, threatening firemen below.

More than two hundred men, women, and children descended the stairs, stumbling over each other in their panic to get out—only to discover that the exterior doors were locked. The underpaid staff proved not much help in evacuating those smoke-choked wretches from the burning building. They were inmates themselves and concerned more with their own survival than with those whom they were paid pennies to serve.

Then the firemen axed open the doors and the nearly naked inmates poured out, over the bodies of those who had been crushed against the locked doors.

J. P. Longard, the fire warden, reported that just when they thought everyone had escaped, they saw a woman on the sixth storey on the north side of the building, leaning out the window and screaming for help. The sixth floor was the hospital ward, where more than fifty people were bedridden. A fire crew raised a ladder, but it fell twenty feet short of reaching the woman. As the firemen watched, the floor gave way, and the woman, still clinging to the window ledge, remained in that position until her head burned off.

A Halifax newspaper reported: "Far above the roar of the flames and the crack of bursting slates, were heard the cries of the wretched patients in the hospital, who were roasting to death. Most of them could not leave their beds, and were, perhaps, stifled by the smoke before the cruel flames reached them, but others were seen to dash themselves against the windows and cling to the sash till their strength was exhausted or their hands burned off and they fell back into the seething caldron of flames."

On the west side of the building, a dozen firemen risked entering, dragging hoses behind them. They climbed to the third floor, and played the streams back and forth, trying to keep the fire in the centre of a room so half a dozen inmates—all in nightshirts and huddled near a window—could escape. Then fire from the floor below burst through the ceiling and filled the room behind them. They swung their hoses around to drive back the flames, and with the inmates in tow, they made their escape.

Only fireman James White was left behind. He ducked low to escape the flames that were flaring up the walls and across the ceiling, and breathed in the air that the fire was drawing along the floor. On hands and knees, he crawled through the choking smoke and under an archway of flames. A blast of smoke stuffed his lungs and stung his eyes. Beneath the smoke and flames, he saw a tiny, terrified face pressed into a corner, with the paint bubbling off the walls around her.

He crawled to that little girl and gathered her under his arm, shielding her with his big body. Then he made for a window, and cleared it of broken glass. He lowered the girl into the outstretched arms of another fireman, then eased himself through the window and dropped onto a ladder.

The fire burned throughout the following day, and smouldered for weeks after. The poor asylum was a total loss.

Of the 343 inmates, 31 had died: 8 men and 23 women.

THE CURING QUALITIES OF A HANGED MAN

In the eighteenth and nineteenth centuries in the Maritimes, the law was indeed the scourge of the wicked. Many went to the gallows for crimes we would consider insignificant, and they—along with convicted cutthroats and thieves—provided Maritimers with a source of entertainment. Hanging day drew large crowds. Not all came to witness the spectacle of an execution. Some stood at the foot of the gallows hoping to get a good look at the hanged man—or better yet, to touch the corpse.

In Great Britain, it was once believed that seeing or touching the corpse of a hanged man was good luck. That belief travelled across the ocean with the early settlers. Some even believed that the corpse possessed the power to cure most diseases.

In 1815, in Charlottetown, Prince Edward Island, Sancho Byers—a black servant and quite possibly a slave—robbed Matilda Bracken of an undisclosed amount of money. A few days later, his brother Peter stole five pounds from James Gibson. Both men were convicted and sentenced to hang.

On hanging day, a large crowd gathered at Gallows Hill. A woman with a tumour on her neck was led through the crowd to the foot of the gallows, so she could be the first to touch the Byers brothers after they were hanged.

Gallows Hill in Charlottetown was located at the highest part of Euston Street, adjacent to Holland Grove. It was customary to bury the bodies of hanged men under the gallows. In 1844, to accommodate a growing city, Gallows Hill had to be levelled off, or as the locals said, "The hill's to be cut down."

Men and women swarmed over Gallows Hill on the day of the excavation, each seeking a souvenir or lucky bone from a hanged man. One boy came home with two bones. His mother was sickly, he said, and he was taking no chances with the cure.

During those early years, Maritimers also believed good luck could be had from watching a man hang. In 1829, Halifax, Nova Scotia, introduced the drop system of execution. This new style of gallows was the trap door type, which allowed the condemned person to drop to a quick death, out of sight of the hundreds of onlookers at the foot of the gallows. It did not go over well with those spectators who hoped to get lucky by seeing a hanged man.

Francis Marvis, a murderer, had the dubious distinction of being the first to try the new system out. He almost seemed pleased to do so. He swaggered to the gallows, and boasted to the crowd that this newfangled hanging machine was nothing without him. Marvis instructed the executioner about adjusting the noose, and even begged to remain unmasked so he could see just how the machine worked.

There was nothing to it. The executioner pounded out the wedge on the trap door, and Marvis dropped out of sight, groaned once, and died.

Spectators disapproved. They booed and hissed, spat on the sheriff, and threw mud and horse dung at the executioner. They wanted to see the hanged man. A pregnant woman shouted wildly, begging for a chance to see Marvis for fear her child would be born blind.

Some had travelled many kilometres for the hanging, and they were disappointed the show had lasted no longer than a minute. As far as the mob was concerned, this newfangled gallows was not a change for the better.

New Brunswick occasionally used another death-machine called the "beam." While the gallows sent its bodies downward, the beam took them straight up.

The beam consisted of a sturdy tree trunk that was upwards of twenty feet long. The butt end was raised about four feet off the ground, and held in place by an iron pin driven through it. A pair of upright planks—one on each side—supported the whole. When the beam was being readied for use, heavy weights were added to the butt end, and a prop held the beam horizontally. At the longer (and lighter) end, the hangman fixed his noose.

The last record of the beam being used was in Saint John in 1870. Justice had to kill one of the city's leading citizens, John Munro, for the murder of his former girlfriend, Margaret Vail, and the child he'd fathered with her.

On the morning of Tuesday, February 15, 1870, Munro walked to the longer end of the beam and had the noose fitted. His executioner then retreated into the jail, where there laid a rope whose other end was tied to the prop. As the town clock finished the last stroke of 8 A.M., the prop fell, and the beam jerked its victim violently upward. In the favourite journalistic phrase of the day, thus John Munro was "launched into eternity."

SEA MONSTERS

In the summer of 1825, Henry Purvis manoeuvred his fishing skiff past McNabs Island in Halifax Harbour, and raised sail for the open sea. He had reached the military fortification at York Redoubt, near the harbour mouth, when he saw it: a long, black snake-like creature zigzagging through the water.

Henry guessed that this creature was about a hundred feet long. And he swore this was no fish story.

Two days later, Captain Gorham and a company of young men and women were taking a carriage ride around the Bedford Basin when they saw a long, black creature basking on the surface of the water. Gorham figured it was upwards of sixty feet long, end to end. As they watched, the creature coiled like a snake, then shot through the water faster than a coastal cutter in a high wind.

Most sea monsters sighted in Halifax Harbour were simply everyday sea creatures never before seen by European settlers. Take the one reported in Halifax in 1752. Townsfolk crowded the waterfront to get a good look a hairy, ox-like creature with a small head and long, dagger-like teeth as it basked on the beach of Georges Island. It was a sea lion. But to those first English settlers, that creature was the strangest thing they had ever seen, and this unfamiliarity made it into a monster.

But unfamiliarity doesn't explain the sea monster sighted in 1825. Henry Purvis was a fisherman, and Gorham was a ship's captain. Both knew the sea, and much of what lived in it, and in separate sightings, both reported seeing the same thing: a long, black, snake-like creature about as thick as a tree trunk.

STRANGE AND UNUSUAL

People were more aware of the natural world in days gone by. They seemed to see more in nature than we do today. They regularly saw more ghosts, and witnessed some of the strangest, most inexplicable things.

According to the *Acadian Recorder* newspaper, on August 2, 1814, more than fifty passengers on the ship *William Heathcote*—which was sailing from St. John's, Newfoundland, to Sydney, Cape Breton—reported seeing the same natural phenomenon. They were off Cape Chat at about noon, when the sun turned a deep blood co-lour. Then, around two thirty, total darkness ensued and continued until sunset.

It was still pitch black again at nine o'clock the next morning. Sailors needed lanterns to see their way around the deck. But by two o'clock in the afternoon, it was as bright as any summer day.

A few weeks later, on August 27, 1814, Captain Hayes—who was returning from Boston to Saint John, New Brunswick, on board the *Majestic*—witnessed the strangest thing. All the crew saw it, too: the outline of a human figure in the sun. At sunrise, the figure was lying flat, but as the sun climbed in the sky, so did the figure, until at noon hour, it stood up straight. As the sun lowered in the sky, the figure seemed to lie down flat.

The following day, the same thing happened. Only this day, the figure looked more like a skeleton, and carried six flags.

Captain Hayes believed this was a bad omen, and thanked his lucky stars when the *Majestic* dropped anchor in Saint John. Several of the crew also thought it was a bad sign, and never went to sea again.

GOVERNOR PARR

In 1925, in broad daylight, a three-mast schooner cut across the bow of an ocean liner then sailed on. In his log, the captain of the ocean liner noted the name of the schooner: the *Governor Parr*. But there was something strange about the schooner, the captain recorded. There were no masts and no rigging, no crewmember was at the wheel, and no one was on deck.

On September 27, 1923, the *Governor Parr* had sailed out of Ingramport, Nova Scotia, captained by Angus Richards. It was bound for South America with a cargo of lumber. But after four days at sea, the schooner ran straight into the jaws of a howling hurricane.

Cross spars and rigging crashed to the deck in a heavy, tangled mass. The ship listed with the weight of the rigging, and in hurricane winds, it would soon capsize. Captain Angus Richards knew that ordering the crew to clear the wreckage could very well send them to their deaths. So he did it himself.

He climbed onto the rigging that hung out over the water, then frantically chopped and chopped, freeing the tangled mass—just as a gigantic wave washed it and the captain further over the side. Yet even then, in that mountain of sea, Captain Richards ordered his crew into the lifeboats, and to keep their heads. "You're in the steamer lanes," he shouted, before going under.

For two days, the crew drifted in the open lifeboats. Then a US Coast Guard cutter, the *Tampa*, sailed past and rescued the crew.

The *Governor Parr* sailed on, following the ocean currents between North and South America, often seen by freighters and liners as it criss-crossed the steamer lanes. It was a hazard to transatlantic shipping. Governments and salvage companies mapped the ship's movements, but were unsuccessful in their efforts to find and destroy her.

Then in October 1925, the *Governor Parr* cut across the bow of that ocean liner that was bound for New York—and was never seen again.

MICE PLAGUE

In Biblical times, God visited ten plagues on Egypt as punishment for keeping the Israelites in bondage. Later, he sent similar plagues on the Israelites to punish them for their sinful ways. So when plague of mice hit Pictou County, Nova Scotia, in 1815, some God-fearing folk claimed God was punishing the county for forty years of sin and hard living.

Mice seemed to cover the earth as far as the eye could see. They were in barns and pig troughs, in cellars and closets, in woodlands and fields. Where the early violets had bloomed the year before, there were now the eyes and noses of millions of mice.

And they were hungry. They ate corn, grain, vegetables, and seed. A Merigomish farmer sowed a field with oats one morning. When he turned around to appreciate the morning's work, there was a sea of mice eating everything he had scattered.

With warm weather, the mice seemed to grow and multiply. They were as large as rats, and their hordes were as thick as a swamp full of mosquitoes.

And that was their undoing. There were so many mice that they raped the land to a wasteland of dusty dirt, and by late summer, there was nothing left for them to eat. The mice died by the thousands. The air was thick with the stink of dead mice. Soon the remaining mice moved to the seacoast to feed on shellfish. And there the tide carried them out to sea.

It was said that in the summer of 1815, fishermen from Cape Breton to the north shore of New Brunswick could gut a fish and find a mouse in its belly.

THE NEW BRUNSWICK– MAINE BOUNDARY DISPUTE

What does Wilhelm, king of the Netherlands, have to do with the New Brunswick–Maine boundary? Keep reading!

Americans and Maritimers have been arguing over that boundary since 1764, when Massachusetts tried to grab a large piece of Nova Scotia land. But it really got down to heavy haggling after the American Revolution. Both sides agreed that the ancient and true boundary was the St. Croix River. The dispute was over which river was the St. Croix.

It took ten years before both sides settled on the river that is called the St. Croix today. Then the dispute was how far upriver the boundary ran. The Maritimers wanted the boundary set at Mars Hill. The Americans didn't.

That's where Wilhelm, king of the Netherlands, comes in. The sides agreed to let Wilhelm, an independent neutral, decide the issue.

Poor Wilhelm! He pored over conflicting maps of the wilderness, and wrestled with names of waterways that only the locals could pronounce, like Chip-et-ne'ti-cook, Me-du'x-ne-keg, and Wool-as-took-pec-ta-waa-g-o-mic.

He wrote his decision in French, the language of diplomacy in the eighteenth century. But then he complicated things: he wanted the northern boundary line to be traced out by the deepest part of a valley—the St. John River. Only he didn't have a French word for this, so he used the German and Dutch one, "Thalweg."

No one knew what he meant. So they argued for another thirteen years.

Finally, in 1842, the Maritimers threw in the towel and gave up the Mars Hill claim, and Maine got a lot of territory that might otherwise have been in New Brunswick.

And by the way, they also agreed that the northern boundary above Grand Falls should be the middle of the St. John River—which is what King Wilhelm had been trying to tell them in the first place.

MAGAZINE EXPLOSION

World War Two was over in the summer of 1945. Most Canadian naval ships steamed for Halifax, Nova Scotia, to unload their dangerous cargoes of torpedoes, depth charges, and anti-aircraft ammunition.

These ships crowded the Halifax Harbour and the Bedford Basin, waiting for their turn to unload onto one of the dozens of lighters—small barges that transported the ammunition to the jetty at the naval magazine.

The barges worked day and night, stacking ammunition on the jetty faster than the dockside crews could store it. Soon the jetty was chockablock with ordinance.

Captain Robertson had the responsibility of directing traffic on the jetty, and he told truckers and work crews where to stack torpedoes and where to pile depth charges. And when a spark set off a series of explosions that would last all night, Captain Robertson was still directing traffic, but now his directions were to get ammunition off the jetty to safety.

Explosions lit up the night sky and filled the air with red, glowing shrapnel. Still Captain Robertson remained at his post, as poised and calm as a traffic cop during Monday morning rush hour. And it's a good thing he did. By moving much of that ammunition to safety, Robinson's individual courage saved Halifax from a second devastating explosion.

PATROL BOAT

During the Second World War, Cape Breton coal fired the engines of Allied ships and supply trains. Coal was as valuable to the war effort as guns and bullets. Like ammunition, coal needed protection from the German U-boats that cruised these Maritime waters.

Small navy patrol boats kept watchful eyes on the harbour mouth, and on the traffic in and out of the port of Sydney. But at night, with bow lights and ships' lanterns strictly prohibited, the patrol boats' eyes turned stone blind in the darkness.

After dark, with the harbour choked with escort ships and huge coal barges, the small patrol boats had their work cut out just staying clear of the movements of these friendly ships. They kept their engines revved, and an eye peeled for large shadows cutting across their bow.

One night, a sailor named William Coughran was down in the engine room of a patrol boat. He could hear the chugging and churning of more than a hundred engines being transmitted through the water. Then one engine got louder and louder—so loud that Coughran, a ship's engineer, could distinguish one of its valves sticking in the cylinder.

He hollered to the watch on deck. But the looming shadow of a coal barge had already crossed the bow, with the steel of its massive hull close behind. All six sailors on the patrol boat's deck jumped for their lives, grabbing the half-raised anchor on the barge and pulling themselves up. Here the six sailors perched until they were rescued at first light, over a kilometre outside the harbour.

Coughran, who was still below deck, grabbed hold of a ship's ladder and held tight. Lucky for him, the patrol boat glanced and slid off the coal barge's hull, then settled into the darkness as though nothing had happened.

THE *CHUBB* AND THE *EMULOUS*

During the War of 1812, thugs and riff-raff often took to the sea for plunder. They preyed on coastal communities that were helpless against their fishing schooners, which were armed with deck cannon and manned by money-hungry sailors. The British navy patrolled the Nova Scotia coastline, on the lookout for these American privateers.

In the spring of 1812, His Majesty's brig the *Emulous* was hunting an American privateer near Liverpool. With thick fog and the chance of running a reef or sandbar, tension on the *Emulous* was high, and nerves were frayed at the prospect of a hand-to-hand fight with the American sailors.

All of a sudden, a sail appeared through the fog off the starboard bow. Captain Herd, commander of the *Emulous*, hailed the passing ship. Not hearing an immediate response, he ordered his crew to fire chain shot. Chain shot consisted of two cannonballs connected by a chain. It effectively cut apart a ship's mast and rigging, rendering the vessel helpless.

No sooner was the cannon fired than a voice called across the water, identifying itself as Captain DeMerique of His Majesty's schooner *Chubb*, a coastal cutter. He too was in pursuit of the American privateer.

Fearing attack, Captain DeMerique had remained silent at Captain Herd's hailing, and his silence cost two sailors their lives. Ebenezer Harrington and John Scott, both from Liverpool, were cut in half by the chain shot.

BLOODY CREEK

Outside Bridgetown, Nova Scotia, peat bogs taint the water in a certain creek a rusty colour. In sunlight, the creek almost looks like it is running with blood. That's one reason early settlers called that run of rusty-looking water Bloody Creek. There's another.

In 1757, Captain Pidgeon and one hundred British redcoats set out from Fort Anne at Annapolis Royal to chase down a company of French soldiers and Mi'kmaq warriors. The British marched along the south side of the Annapolis River for two days. They could have marched forever through the thick forest, bogs, and tall river grass without seeing another living soul, let alone the French soldiers.

About eight kilometres into their return march, they crossed a log bridge over a small creek. Shots rang out from all sides. Several British soldiers fell with that first volley. Then a second brought down a few more.

The ambush confused and befuddled the British. Half crossed the bridge; half took cover on the opposite bank.

Captain Pidgeon led an assault to reunite his patrol. There came another volley from those in ambush, and several more British soldiers fell dead into the running water. Now Pidgeon rallied his troops, re-crossed the bridge, and retreated to Fort Anne, leaving behind thirty-six British soldiers dead in the water of what would come to be called Bloody Creek.

A PLACE FURTHER ON

Around 1800, Joseph and Priscilla Mosher settled at the upper Kennetcook River in central Nova Scotia, on a piece of land wedged between the high tide of the Minas Basin and the hard rock spine of the Rawdon Hills. The Minas Basin is a sixty-kilometre-long, trumpet-shaped body of water off the Bay of Fundy. From bell to mouthpiece, the basin funnels through a roaring tide, which rises upwards of thirty feet and leaves in its ebb a cookie-cutter coastline of red sandstone and shale. Pressing hard to the basin are the Rawdon Hills, a worn-down mountain range loaded with limestone and gypsum, and deeply veined with gold.

The Kennetcook is hardly a majestic river, but it flows year-round with enough water to turn a mill wheel. For early pioneers looking to farm the rich, loamy soil of this valley, a river that could turn a wheel to grind their grain and saw their lumber was a river worth settling beside.

So it was along this river that Joseph and Priscilla Mosher hacked a homestead from a forest fat with white pine and hemlock. They hand-turned the rich earth that God had fertilized and watered with time, rot, and freshets. And they hunkered against winters colder than Billy-be-goddamned, and swatted their way through the mosquito-driven misery of summer.

They hardened their bodies by simply living, stacking hard work against every hour of every day. They chopped trees, pulled stumps, and used a peavey to move logs in place to build a cabin. Then they scattered seed for a field crop of wheat. They cut and hewed what they lived in; sowed and harvested what they ate; skinned, tanned, spun, and wove what they wore. They did so on their own land— land for which they held a deed, a government deed to the fields and forest over which they shed their blood for the sake of their children and their children's children.

It was off that land that Joseph and Priscilla gathered and threshed grain by hand. And it was over that land that Joseph walked thirteen kilometres to grind the grain into flour at Densmore Mills on the Noel Shore.

The road to the mill was little more than a rocky path through the woods—not much good for a dray cart or a wagon. In late summer and fall, Joseph slung bags of grain on his back and lugged them to the mill. Each bag held one and a half bushels of grain and weighed about seventy pounds. That's a sizable load for a man to carry on his back for thirteen kilometres.

Joseph would carry one bag a kilometre, and then set it on a stump. He then walked back for the second bag, and carried it a kilometre beyond the first. This leapfrog method of toting his grain tripled the distance he travelled. It took the better part of a day, and the return trip with a load of ground flour took just as long.

It was hard slugging the grain on that rough path, and lonely too. Joseph would lug one heavy bag, then breath easy as he returned to fetch the other, all the time scanning the woods for danger—and thinking, thinking, thinking.

Lord knows what Joseph Mosher thought about. Most likely he did what most of us do when walking in the deep woods or paddling a lake: clear our minds of big ideas, and let a scatter of mental images play peekaboo with our feelings. It's not quite daydreaming; it's more like thinking in a haphazard sort of way. Sometimes we fix on one image, and feel all around the edges for a nub of truth that sometimes shows itself as a hope, a fear, a love. Or sometimes the image goes blurry with the long desire to squeeze more out of life than just time spent.

Joseph and Priscilla Mosher planned their future the way Joseph had planned the plank bridge he built over the Kennetcook River—straight, firm, and even. But they were no fools. They knew long before they had burned the brambles from their fields, and buried a broadaxe in the butt end of His Majesty's mast pine, that their lives would twist with hard times the way green lumber twists in the summer sun. They were fifth-generation pioneer stock, so they knew the dangers they faced while farming and raising ten kids in the shadows of a wild, dreamy, and oftentimes cruel forest.

From his father, James Mosher, Joseph had learned of the dangers earlier settlers had faced. On many nights, his father had told of the long-ago days when three Moshers—Hugh, Daniel, and John—from Manchester, England, first set foot in the New World at Rhode Island. Was that in the 1650s? The 1660s? Who could recall? After a hundred years of hard living, the family's memory had become unreliable. Table talk of history easily blurred one year into the next, and sometimes mixed up the details in the lives of those who had gone before. Sometimes a son's name got pinned on a father's deed, or a wife was remembered as the widow of the wrong brother. Sometimes a child went nameless, or a stillbirth was forgotten.

Of course, there were church records to set order to the details. But what storyteller runs to church on a winter's night, when the fire and family offer so much comfort? Besides, the scrawl of names in a church record is naked of life, unconnected to gladness and pain. It lies on the page as brittle as the paper itself. Names alone are factual but faceless. They lack feeling, and facts without feeling make a corpse of history.

So James Mosher told his son of the long ago by remembering how it had been told to him. Sometimes he made up what he could not remember, or what his own father or grandfather had forgotten to say. Sometimes he stuffed the names of his ancestors with his own heart and told the truth of their lives infused with what he felt himself.

Most often, James Mosher told about selling all he owned in Rhode Island and coming to Nova Scotia. What drew James Mosher, and two thousand other Yankee settlers, to Nova Scotia was the lure of land—rich land that was less crowded and more promising than any in all of New England. They sought land that a government proclamation in 1758 had made free for the taking.

Some called these newcomers "New England Planters," after the old English word for "colonist." Others called them "New England scavengers" because the land they settled had once belonged to the Acadians. The newcomers, however, simply called themselves lucky for the chance to settle some of the most fertile land created by God.

James Mosher and family were one of the first in line for passage to Nova Scotia aboard the ship *Lydia*. James went to the wharf at Newport, Rhode Island, and boarded the ship with good credentials: he was a millwright, a man who knew how to build mill wheels and machinery for grinding, sawing, and spinning. James Mosher was a plum to a new settlement. A strong back might guarantee a man's place during the gruff days of wilderness clearing, but know-how with machinery added lustre to his name when the clearing was done and the farming began. It also helped put money into his pocket and bread on his table.

In 1760, twenty-three Rhode Island settlers and their families landed at the mouth of the Avon River on the Minas Basin. Almost at once, they mapped out a thousand acres per family on the east side of the river, and started clearing the land and grubbing a future from the soil. They sweated the day away at this back-bending work. They blurred their minds of thought, and focused their instincts on nothing else but felling this tree and hauling that stump.

Some stayed right where they had landed, and called the place Newport; others pushed on. James Mosher was one who saw sunshine and clover beyond the settlement on the Avon River. He saw his future in the land further on: untamed land where a man could swing his elbows freely, where he and his wife could lay out their long desire for a peaceful life, and count the stars—millions of them—untroubled by the glow from too many nearby cabins.

With his land grant stuffed under his shirt, James and his family set out for paradise. They loaded a raft with all they owned, and poled down the Avon and then up the Kennetcook as far as the river would allow. Then they trudged past sucking bogs and the gnarly undergrowth of bluegrass meadows, until they reached a place where eelgrass waved in the wind and thick forest reached back from the mud-slick riverbanks; where the sky broke blue and the sun gleamed on the streaks of birch among the dark green of the hillsides.

This was the place he would call home; the place generations of Moshers would scrap for and cling to; the place that would bear his name (Mosherville); the place that his son Joseph and Joseph's young wife, Priscilla Greno, would one day leave so they could settle a patch of land at another place further on.

Joseph and Priscilla shaped the land they settled at Upper Kennetcook according to the lives they lived and the love they shared. They built a round-log cabin with moss caulking. It was raw and rugged, but swept with care. Joseph and Priscilla laboured long, they laboured hard, and they laboured together. They cut, chopped, planted, and harvested side by side. Of course, Joseph had his work—men's work—like teaming and ploughing, hunting wild game, and logging firewood. Stacking it was part of Priscilla's work—women's work. It was no easier, just different. She fed the hog and milked the cow, churned and dressed butter (sometimes 11 3/4 pounds in a day), hoed the garden, hilled potatoes, and cooked most of what they and their ten kids ate.

There were no harps playing to their accomplishments, and no violins. The Moshers moved to the rhythm of their own lives, and worked to the beat of the simple world around them. They sang simple songs too, about life and love, happiness and misfortune.

They expressed their love in much the same way: simply. There were no hearts and flowers. No special day on the calendar for sweetness. No store-bought words to say what most often need not be said. They showed their love in the life they shared: in the sweat of their brows by day and their sore muscles come evening; in a nod or a wink by the fire; in ten kids conceived in their marriage bed.

So in 1813, when Priscilla took sick, Joseph felt her wheezy breathing through every nerve in his body. His face stretched with worry as she rasped and hacked to clear the consumption from her lungs. And his knees weakened when two weeks of sweet wine and honey brought her no relief.

The nearest doctor was thirty-seven kilometres away in Mosherville, over a root-ribbed, broken-stone path and a swollen river. To prepare for the journey, Joseph dragged one of the children's featherbeds from the cabin to the backyard. He rigged the bed with two birch poles, laced strips of leather around the poles, and then around himself, strapping his shoulders and chest with what looked like a horse harness. Next, he blanketed Priscilla in the bed, and cushioned her head for the bumpiest ride you can imagine. Finally, he hauled and hauled. For thirty-seven kilometres Joseph hauled that bed with Priscilla in it. He groaned against the weight, and sweated buckets with each kilometre. The leather harness chafed his skin as raw as butchered beef.

Priscilla coughed on the bumps and wheezed on the downgrades. She sweated from fever as much as Joseph sweated from work. At the riverbank, she hacked and spit and bawled, and for the first time in thirteen years of married life, Priscilla Mosher begged her husband to ease off his effort and give her six minutes of soft comfort.

By the time they reached Mosherville, Priscilla knew the shape, size, and general location of every tree root and boulder along that path. She knew, too, just how much her man loved her.

Priscilla survived the trip there and back—but not for long. Despite doctoring and prayers and a whole lot of rest, Priscilla Mosher—once a woman all beef to the heels, the offspring of good pioneering stock, with thick blood and a strong, unbending spirit—wasted to a shadow of herself and opened her arms to death.

Joseph Mosher held a wake for Priscilla in their home, and buried her in a plot of ground overlooking the Kennetcook River. Some take the death of a loved one harder than others. Some lose a little of themselves with the death of the person they love, and some lose a lot. For the next year, maybe two, Joseph struggled for a while, then he gave in to sorrow and the randomness of life.

There are those who say a woman takes death better than a man. They say a woman understands more than a man could ever know about how death grows within us as we live, and that dying is just another way of giving birth. Maybe that's why Priscilla's death sent cracks into Joseph's spirit; why he broke up housekeeping, sold his land, and scattered the kids among his and Priscilla's families. Maybe he just had a man's way of looking at life and taking in death. Maybe her passing promised nothing for Joseph Mosher—maybe for him, Priscilla's death was the beginning of the end.

Joseph was forty-four when Prescilla died. For the next dozen years or so, Joseph kicked about Hants County along the Kennetcook River, taking odd jobs as a carpenter and millwright—a trade he had picked up from his father.

Around 1845, Joseph manufactured a pair of grinding stones for a mill at the mouth of the Noel River. He spent the better part of the fall chiselling those stones to turn true. When he was done, he axled them together and set them out in the mud off Indian Point, to be picked up by a boat which would sail them up the Minas Basin. The next day, a winter storm blew across the basin, packing a blast of Arctic air so fierce it could have blown the hair off a dog and frozen the milk in a cow's udder. The grinding stones froze in the mud—so firmly that a boat equipped with a greased hurdy-gurdy and the muscle of a dozen men could not budge it.

New Year's came and went. The stones stayed put. And the settlers on the Noel River, whose barns were loaded with grain they could not grind, went hungry.

Then in March, the weather changed. A southerly wind seemed to stray off the Gulf Stream current, and warm its way up the eastern seaboard and into the Minas Basin. Right behind that warm air was one wild rhapsody of a storm, the first cousin to a hurricane. It blew for one whole day and one whole night, unfroze the basin, and drove the ice—and anything untethered along the shore—into the squeeze of Cobequid Bay. The wind and the tide reshaped the sandstone coast around the basin and dragged boulders for kilometres—and the grinding stones too. They rolled with the wind and waves, and fetched up on the beach at the mouth of the Noel River, within thirty feet of the mill for which they had been intended.

The settlers' jaws dropped at the sight of those stone wheels. God may have been slow to answer their prayers, but when He finally made up his mind to do so, He worked fast. But not much faster than it took Joseph Mosher to sleigh across country, set the stones in the mill, and gear them down for grinding. Joseph became the miller.

He milled on the Noel River for several years after that. By the time he turned seventy, his back had played out. His kids, who lived along the Avon River, took turns caring for him.

Joseph continued to earn his keep by husking and grinding barley with a mortar and pestle. He did it the old Mi'kmaq way. He cut a hardwood log to about three feet long, then bored and burned a round, smooth hole into it. The hole measured twelve inches wide and fifteen deep. Joseph would sit for hours, pounding the barley until he had enough for a hearty soup to feed eight, sometimes ten people. As he worked, he would listen to the sounds of his grandchildren and great-grandchildren, the sounds of the countryside—and to a new sound drifting across the Avon River. There was something hurried about that new sound, something that suggested rushing into a future that had no place for a man his age. Some said that sound would beget a spirit of enterprise, which would then beget a bright and glorious future. They said it promised prosperity for the generations of Moshers to come.

Joseph thought about the hope in those words as he went on pounding the barley. If the words proved true, then all that had gone before—the fear and the fighting, the hard living and the dying, the kindling of young love and the deep hurt from losing it—if the words proved true, if the sound he had heard would beget a bright and glorious future and provide for the next generations a good living at a place further on, then all that had gone before had been worth it.

On August 16, 1859, Joseph "took the bowel or summer complaint." He had rectal cancer. He lived another three days. They say that as he lay dying, he heard that strange sound for the last time—the sound of a railroad.

His family buried him in the Lockhart/Nelson Cemetery, which sat on land between the farms of Evelyn Leighton and Stephen Fitzgerald in Mosherville. His tombstone reads: "In Memory of Joseph Mosher, Who Departed this Life August 19, 1859." Joseph was ninety-one.

BEARS

(BJG)

Lawfield was a Queens County community that lay south of the St. John River. Now abandoned, the land becoming part of Base Gagetown, it was populated in the early twentieth century by British immigrants with family names such as Law, Lindsay, Hughes, and McMinn. A six-kilometre-long woods road linked it to the town of Gagetown.

One spring evening around 1910, a man named Lindsay had business at McKinney's store in Gagetown. The road there was so familiar to him, he didn't start off until nearly dusk. By the halfway mark, darkness had almost fallen—but not so much that he couldn't recognize an even darker shape that suddenly reared up before him.

Lindsay knew bears, and could recognize the smell of them. He knew that trying to outrun one on level ground was folly. And he knew that when a bear stands, it means to attack.

Bears seldom kill with their teeth. Instead, they have claws that extend four to five inches—claws as sharp as steel, and nearly as hard. With a human victim, a bear's technique is to hug him, raise a hind foot, extend its claws, and disembowel him. It is not a pleasant way to die.

Lindsay reached for the only weapon he had: a jackknife. When the bear tried to hug him, Lindsay raised the open knife, and made the last motion he ever expected to make: with every ounce of strength desperation could muster, he brought the knife down on the bear's head.

Oddly, the animal's arms dropped away, and it slunk off into the nearby woods.

For the next three kilometres, Lindsay beat all speed records, and arrived at McKinney's store exhausted. When he recovered, no one doubted his story.

McKinney kept Lindsay all night. The next morning, several men armed with rifles joined Lindsay for the return trip.

Lindsay knew the road so well that he could show them almost the exact spot where the encounter had happened. The men expected to find nothing. But there, not twenty feet from the spot Lindsay showed them, lay the bear—stone dead, with the handle of Lindsay's jackknife sticking out of its skull.

THE AUBURN SYSTEM

W. H. Roach was a magistrate with the city of Halifax, and commissioner of the Halifax jail. The jail was called the Bridewell, after the city of Bridewell in England where a notorious penitentiary was located. Roach also wore another hat: he was a Halifax merchant, and principal supplier of foodstuffs and supplies to the Bridewell. It was a parasitic arrangement, and Roach was the parasite.

On December 8, 1834, an unnamed source leaked information to the Halifax grand jury (the body that oversaw the execution of the city's bylaws and the management of the city's institutions), reporting shady dealings at the Bridewell. It accused W. H. Roach of selling the jail flour of inferior quality.

The grand jury sent Henry Misnemity, Edward Kennedy, S. Donavan, and Edward Lawson to investigate. They returned with a scathing report.

Mrs. O'Brien, the matron of the Bridewell, testified that flour from Roach was always of mixed quality, and was comprised mostly of coarsely ground Indian meal (cornmeal). Indian meal cost less to produce, and it filled up a barrel a lot faster. Mrs. O'Brien noticed this only after weighing one of the flour barrels and discovering it was sixteen pounds short.

Her husband, the jailer, complained that Roach was lining his own pockets with the expense money for the Bridewell. Roach's latest invoice had totalled fifty-six pounds and nineteen shillings, yet the goods received were valued at only seven pounds.

The investigating committee dug deeper. Money for beds and bedclothes had been expensed by Roach, but not purchased, and prisoners were sleeping uncovered on the damp earth. A woodshed was used to stable Roach's horse, while the firewood was left exposed in the jail yard. There was more. At public expense, John Gilmore, a prisoner and a shoemaker, had made boots and shoes for Roach's family and for the family of a friend of his. A bathing machine and some buckets for the jail ended up in Mr. Roach's home, and several prisoners—D. Hefferman, John Cain, and Patrick Walsh—worked almost exclusively for Roach's business.

The committee, now greatly suspicious, ordered that the account books for the Bridewell be produced. D. S. Clark, the clerk of the peace, refused. So did John Jennings, the collector of poor and county rates. Both ducked behind the legal refuge of "Custos rotulorum," which dated back to the fourteenth century. They claimed that as keepers of the public accounts, they were not subject to the orders of their inferiors—namely the grand jury.

Clearly Clark and Jennings were hiding evidence contained in the public accounts. And they were shielding high-ranking people who would be incriminated.

Despite this refusal, the grand jury had enough evidence to recommend that His Majesty's Council change the entire system of tax collection and treasury record-keeping. As for W. H. Roach, the grand jury recommended that council not pay his expense claims.

And that was it. No forcing Clark and Jennings to come clean with the public accounts; no charges of fraud and embezzlement; no drawn-out court case that exposed the shenanigans of other magistrates, who the grand jury accused of being "aware of their own secrets." And there was no public naming of names. The grand jury simply itemized what it called "abuses and nuisances," and left it at that.

Even then, public bodies were reluctant to investigate and publicly report on their own misdeeds. And when they did, they conveniently swept it under the rug, much like they do today.

However, this innocuous grand jury investigation into the mismanagement of public funds at the Halifax Bridewell opened up a can of worms.

The following year (1835), Joseph Howe published in his newspaper, the *Novascotian*, a letter alleging that magistrates "had by one stratagem or another, taken from the pockets of the people…a sum that would exceed in the gross amount of £30,000." That allegation resulted in Howe being charged with libel, for which he successfully defended himself in court, launching him on a political career that would forever change the face of the Nova Scotia government with sweeping political reform.

At the same time, as a result of following up on the leaked information about W. H. Roach's fraud and mismanagement, the grand jury took a closer look at jail conditions. After a nauseating inspection of the Halifax Bridewell, the grand jury recommended to the Supreme Court that the facility should be closed on December

31, 1835, due to lack of funds. The roof leaked, and the walls were so flimsy that the previous year, sixteen prisoners had pushed their way through and escaped.

The grand jury continued: "...most prisoners suffered from want of clothing, some having no stockings, others only one, others without a jacket to protect them." At night, they had "a few ragged blankets barely averaging one to each individual and those swarming with vermin to a degree beyond belief." The stench from a swamp of human waste in the lower cells could turn a millstone black. Had it not been for lavender-scented handkerchiefs, the grand jury would have halted their inspection on the first floor.

Most prisoners suffered from one illness or another. Only four were able to work—barely. One prisoner, Rodgers, had "a loathsome disease of a most virulent description." Dr. Stirling, the prison physician, had ignored Rodgers's condition for more than six weeks.

The grand jury's conclusion was that such a facility challenged most everyone's sense of justice. "It is as disgraceful as it is useless... merely affording a miserable refuge for the victim, the most abandoned and wretched outcasts of society."

No one took the grand jury's recommendations seriously—not the Supreme Court, and not the prison commissioner, John Albro, who had not inspected the cells in over six months. The Bridewell's doors remained open, to the dismay of the prisoners, who were serving their sentences in living conditions the grand jury called "revolting to the feelings of humanity."

The following year, the grand jury again recommended closing the Halifax jail. This time, they suggested replacing it with "a provincial institution that punished and reformed, one that separated prisoners into individual cells, and spared first offenders from the corrupting influence of hardened convicts." The penal system the grand jury had in mind was called the Auburn System.

Disciples of this new approach to incarceration claimed they had an understanding of the criminal mind. They proposed that hard work and silence would transform hardened criminals into "contrite pilgrims in search of their lost characters." They pinned their conclusions on the simple belief that "thieves and murderers, though degraded by their offences, are yet the subjects of moral influence and elevation."

Salvation through hard work and silence was not a new idea. The Cistercian Monks have been doing it successfully since the Middle Ages. However, there is a difference between a monk signing up for a cloistered life and a hardened criminal accepting it as part of his punishment. For one thing, criminals lacked the same spiritual motivation as Cistercian monks.

Nevertheless, the Quaker divines in Pennsylvania had adopted the Auburn system as a means of criminal reform in 1790, and in 1840, following the grand jury's recommendation, the Nova Scotia House of Assembly did the same for the new provincial penitentiary it planned to build on the Northwest Arm. The theory was simple: exhaust a sinner through hard work, then turn him back to God through self-contemplation.

By 1844, the prison's cloistered walls welcomed forty-three convicts: twenty-four thieves and robbers, thirteen military deserters, and six pirates from the ship *Saladin*. People lined the streets to watch the county's prisoners march out from the Bridewell's diseased cells and into the new penitentiary's whitewashed walls.

The prisoners marvelled at the clean floors, individual cells, full meals, and striped uniforms. What they didn't expect was the hard work and discipline that came with the benefits of the Auburn system.

Daily attendance at religious service was a must. So was absolute silence: "For it is by a rigid adherence to this rule only that isolation of the convicts, and thereby their safety and possible reformation can be secured."

Liquor was forbidden. So were singing, whistling, swearing, and smoking—even for the guards. Prisoners had to keep themselves clean and tidy. And of course, they had to work.

In the first six months, the convicts built benches, furniture, closets for their cells, and outbuildings in the prison yard, as well as breaking up 140 tons of granite stones, which the prison governor then sold in town. The board of directors boasted that among the prisoners, three had apprenticed as carpenters, two as tailors, one as a shoemaker, and one as a blacksmith. Seven had worked as labourers, and three women had been domestics. Other early events at the prison included one man escaping, another's time expiring, two more holding pardons for good behaviour, and the *Saladin* pirates being hanged.

Not bad for the first six months. However, once the new prison had a few years under its belt, discipline and order deteriorated. The guards and prison governor became as criminal-minded as the inmates, and they engaged in the same underhanded shenanigans as W. H. Roach had a decade earlier. They cheated prisoners of their daily food rations, bought bad food cheap, and pocketed the difference. They also profited from the daily work of the inmates.

In the 1850s, prison-keeper George Cuddahy became too familiar with the prisoners. On one occasion, he oversaw a work gang of prisoners who were haying a nearby field. Cuddahy lay down under a shade tree, and fell asleep with a loaded gun at his side. Less than a week later, he was discovered drunk in his quarters. That time, the keys to the lock-up went missing, and an inmate named Pratt escaped with a double-barrelled shotgun.

In turn, the prisoners rebelled against the strict regulations. Solitary confinement—during which a prisoner was put in a dark cell, clapped in leg irons, and given only bread and water for rations—soon became the hardened criminal's badge for nonconformity. In October 1844, prisoner number sixteen went into solitary for swearing at a guard. The following day, the guard, John Fitzpatrick, opened the cell door to check on the prisoner, and felt a rush of air past his head. Number sixteen had broken a leg off the bedstead to use as a club. Had the prisoner's leg irons not held him close to the far wall, John Fitzpatrick would have been a dead man.

By 1867, conditions in this formerly model penitentiary had become as wretched as those in the old Bridewell. That's when James Burns, a political rabble-rouser, came on the scene. Burns was a tightly bound snarl of complaints, imprisoned for assaulting a Halifax alderman. This minor offence got him padlocked in the provincial penitentiary—a crafty way for Halifax officials to rid the streets of a social radical parading around town, demanding a descent living for the workingman.

If the officials thought Burns was a nuisance outside of prison, they now had the devil to pay with him behind bars. Within two days, Burns had fifty prisoners banging on their tables and complaining that the food was unfit to eat. Next they threw their food on the floor—and then all hell broke loose. They smashed tables, chairs, and windows; then, armed with chair legs and chains, they scuffled with the guards, grabbed the keys, and escaped the cellblock into the open air of the prison yard.

Wildness surged, fuelled by a beefy, blood-throbbing pressure to destroy. The prisoners tore down a shed, then a stable. Next they set fire to the guardhouse and started tearing clapboard from the governor's quarters.

James Burns was at the head of this mob, flushed with anger—a little man astride madness and chaos.

Soldiers from the Citadel soon arrived. On the prison governor's orders, all twenty soldiers aimed their muskets and fired at once. A single blast of gun smoke and lead struck a single target, for a single purpose: to silence the ringleader, James Burns.

The other prisoners quickly surrendered.

So much for the model prison with its system of silence and hard work guiding desperate men and women to salvation. It worked for a time—a short time—and then human nature took over, as it always does. Nevertheless, the Auburn system was a start in the right direction, emphasizing prisoner reformation over pure punishment.

ELECTIONS

In earlier years, elections in Nova Scotia and New Brunswick were hardly orderly, non-violent exercises in democratic rights. Some were downright slugfests.

On March 18, 1788, the entire Halifax grand jury (the governing body of the municipality) resigned because of an election riot the previous month. The *Nova Scotia Gazette* reported armed men parading the streets and attacking peaceful citizens for not supporting their party. And Reverend Mather Byles recorded this in a letter to his sisters in Boston: "From February 20th to the 22nd, the Town distracted by the Rage of Electioneering and Violence of Party. There were many drunken mobs, one Life lost and much other Mischief done."

Someone had passed out handbills denouncing the government, and that touched off a powder keg of political sentiment. A man (the *Gazette* does not name him) rushed out of Laycock's Tavern on the beach and clubbed one of the leaflet distributors, cracking open his skull. Others spilled from the tavern and marched the streets, knocking heads and bullying bystanders to support the government.

Benjamin Mulberry and his son, Holmes, supported those opposed to the governing party. Both suffered such severe beatings that the boy almost died.

Nearly thirty years later, in June 1819, three petitions landed on the desk of the clerk of the Nova Scotia House of Assembly. All complained about the same thing: the general election that had been held on May 24.

That election was hardly a lesson in democracy. Voting in the Halifax Township turned into a brawl, complete with election shenanigans that would make modern practices—such as stuffing ballot boxes and voting the graveyard—look trite.

It was a day of political speeches and heavy drinking. The candidates were John Albro, John Pryor, and George Grassie. Tom Maynard, the High Sheriff, supervised the election from a six-foot-square platform in the market square. The candidates stood beside him. After registering their names, voters climbed the hustings and declared their choices in loud voices, so the large crowd gathered before the platform could hear. There was no secret ballot, no way to hide one's vote from those in the crowd who preferred to vote with their fists rather than their voices, no way to duck the eyes of the bullies that John Albro had hired to force voters to declare for him.

One can only imagine casting a ballot in public, as one of Albro's men stood alongside and slapped his open hand with a nightstick. The Nova Scotia election of 1819 was no place for sissies.

It was no place for teetotallers either. Liquor started flowing at sun-up, and continued well after curfew. Most voters reached the polls on wobbly pins, with their clothes rumpled and muddy. Some had cracked skulls from drunken election brawls; others had bloody noses.

Most expected a close race, but few expected that it would come down to the wire—certainly not John Bain and Temple Piers, who kept a running score, and counted all three candidates as dead even by late afternoon. The sun was low in the sky when Doctor Keegan and Ed Douchet, both supporters of George Grassie, climbed the platform to cast their votes. Many in the crowd shouted their praise; many others threatened their lives.

Doc Keegan leaned forward to shake hands with several men in the front row. As he did so, the High Sheriff made the most of the doc's distraction. With the western sky still aglow, the High Sheriff fired his musket to signal that the sun had set and the polls had closed. Everyone seemed to catch a collective breath. In that short silence, Tom Maynard called the vote a tie, and declared John Albro, the incumbent, the winner.

Suddenly there were more sticks and fists swinging than there was room to duck. Temple Piers and John Bain both went home with bruised knuckles and their eyes swollen shut.

It took weeks for the dust to settle. Finally, based on evidence that several men who had voted for John Albro did so unlawfully, Thomas Haliburton put forward a motion to the House of Assembly declaring George Grassie the winner. The House voted twenty-one to eleven in favour.

Little changed in Nova Scotia electioneering over the next decade. The Brandy Election of 1830 was a one-week brawl. Hired thugs on the government side bashed the brains of the young idealists who stood in opposition. The government used muscle to keep Beamish Murdock and his supporters away from the polls.

Murdock and his cronies—Thomas Haliburton, Alex Stewart, and Joseph Howe—were known as the "beardless boys": young, liberal reformers who wanted to change the current system of government by the few to government by the many. They sought to wrest power from the old Loyalist oligarchy (the Family Compact) and give it to the people. On the surface, the election was fought over a four-pence tax on brandy. But at its core, the real issue was a principle of power.

There were many Nova Scotians who doubted they would be any worse off being governed by mob rule instead of being ruled over by a gang of aristocrats. But there were many more who were threatened by the insecurity of change, and by the clubs and brick-bats of the government thugs.

In the end, the government won. The fighting had become so bloody and so continuous that Beamish Murdock conceded defeat in order to stop it. Nevertheless, reform had a foothold, and before long, the old-style politics of Family Compact came to an end.

New Brunswick had its share of electoral donnybrooks, but none so wild as the one that has come to be called "The Fighting Election of 1843." This was a bitter, no-holds-barred feud between two politi-cal bosses and business rivals from the north and south sides of the Miramichi River.

Joseph Cunard, of Cunard family fame, bossed politics on the south side—the Chatham side—the way he bossed everything else: ruthlessly. He was a timber merchant and shipbuilder, a monster of a man who tipped the scales at over two hundred pounds. He had a big voice too, and could be heard shouting orders to his mill workers from one end of Chatham to the other. Joe Cunard liked things his way, and most of the time, that's just what he got.

The only man to get in Big Joe's way was Alexander Rankin, a strong-willed lumber baron from Douglastown. They quarrelled over timber rights, mill reserves, and the election of 1843.

Northumberland County had only two representatives in the New Brunswick legislature, and Joe Cunard wanted both of them in his back pocket. So did Alex Rankin: his lumber and mill businesses depended on having a favourable voice in Fredericton. Their feud finally came to blows during a by-election for one of those two seats.

Few cared who the actual candidates were. Most people knew they were voting for either Joseph Cunard or Alexander Rankin. Polling was to be held in Newcastle (the shire town) one day, and then in other towns, including Chatham, on successive days.

Rankin commanded more than fifty able-bodied men, whose sole purpose was to prevent Cunard sympathizers from voting. Most of these were mill workers and lumbermen who knew the business end of an axe handle.

Cunard recruited nearly a thousand goons to do his bidding. They roamed both sides of the river, armed with stones, sticks, chunks of coal, and whatever else would split open the heads of anyone who dared to vote for Rankin's man.

There were bloody skirmishes and hit-and-run raids on both sides of the river. Voters flip-flopped from one candidate to the other, depending on whose gang of thugs was hammering on their front doors.

Then came Election Day in Chatham—the "Day of Siege," the newspapers called it. A rumour cruised up and down the Miramichi that the Rankin thugs intended to march into Chatham, turn any Cunard supporters out of doors, and burn down their houses.

When Cunard caught wind of Rankin's plan, he ordered that a barricade be built to protect Chatham. His men threw together a fortification constructed of fourteen-inch-square timbers, and armed with cannons loaded with scrap iron and spikes.

And then they waited.

Sure enough, the Rankin boys came sailing down river in nine separate vessels. They reached the Chatham wharf, and stood off shore while they sized up the situation. It didn't look good. They were vastly outnumbered and severely outgunned.

So they sailed on, and let the election chips fall where they may.

Rankin's man, Ambrose Street, won the seat in the legislature. But his victory did nothing to quell the bitter animosity between Newcastle and Chatham—a feeling that still barbs the tongue on both sides of the river.

Not long after the election of 1843, the New Brunswick legislature passed a bill granting Northumberland County four seats, in order "to avoid future warfare."

HOPE FOR WOMEN

On March 14, 1784, Rebecca Byles wrote a letter to her aunts in Boston, telling them that girls in Halifax were much better educated than boys. Boys had no need for an advanced education, she said. After all, most of them (and here she meant the sons of the gentry) were destined for the army and navy. They had no need of "knowledge or honesty." They just needed to know how "to dance, make a genteel bow, fill up a printed message card, and sign a receipt."

Since women were better educated, Rebecca reasoned, "In a few years I expect to see women fill the most important Offices in Church and State."

Rebecca Byles wasn't far wrong. It just took many more years than she had anticipated.

"ALGERINES"

In its early days, Saint John, New Brunswick, was divided into two parts—the main town on the east side of the harbour, and a smaller one—an entirely separate community on the west known as West Saint John. And never the twain did meet—at least not on friendly terms.

On January 14, 1837, one of Saint John's disastrous fires broke out. Captain Levinge, a British soldier of the Forty-third Regiment, told about what happened in his diary.

It was a bitter night. A gale blew out of the northwest, and the thermometer showed that it was -22° Celsius. The fire leapt from one wooden building to the next so quickly that by the time Captain Levinge and the troops arrived, confusion and flames were in command everywhere.

Some householders threw their valuables from their windows. Others grabbed an armful and ran. And a gang of sturdy men "rescued" from a threatened wharf nearly two hundred barrels of rum—a ship's cargo.

Levinge described how one of these fellows—exhausted from heaving brimming rum barrels to shore—seated himself on a wheelbarrow in a stunned state. No sooner did he sit down than one of the few men working the fire hoses played a stream of water over him.

Before he could get his senses and muscles working, he was locked like a mummy in an icy shroud and couldn't move.

A friend wheeled him along the waterfront in search of help—and he darn near scared holy mercy out of the soldiers and fire crews as his muffled voice groaned from inside the ice sculpture.

A firefighter grabbed an axe and, with the skill of a woodcarver, chipped the man out of the suit of ice.

Meanwhile the fire raged, and householders continued to toss their belongings from upstairs windows. That made for a great night for the Westsiders. They had crossed the harbour out of curiosity, and now they hurried back with their arms and rowboats full of valuables. Someone spotted the thievery and shouted, "Pirates!"

But Captain Levinge called them something different. He knew all about the Algerians in Africa who pillaged helpless ships that sailed warily past the Algerian coast. Captain Levinge got the name a little twisted, but it was close enough.

"Al-ger-é-ens!" he yelled.

It became a nickname that stuck. For years thereafter, a Westsider venturing over to Saint John could expect to be hooted back with the cry, "G'wan home, ya Algerine!"

THE GRAVE OF BURIED HOPES

Decades of disappointment make people gullible to promises of glory. They easily become prey to fast-talking sharpers, two-bit schemers, and flim-flam artists.

Ever since the days when Confederation fitted the coffin lid over Nova Scotia's economic mastery, the province has flirted with one bamboozler after another. Nova Scotians are all ears when it comes to overblown promises of economic resurrection—whether from gold, coal, oil, or now natural gas. Even today, high-tech talk has them counting money they don't yet have, and the over-hyped rebirth of shipbuilding has them spending it.

One could almost say the circle of hope and disappointment has become a Nova Scotian way of life. Many Nova Scotians would probably disagree—but if you posed that question to those living around East Dalhousie and in the settlement of Crossburn a hundred years ago, they would probably squeeze their faces tight and nod sadly. Back then the economic salvation in that neck of the woods was going to be copper.

Crossburn has always been the last settlement on a dead-end road. But in the early 1900s, with the discovery of copper, Crossburn's prospects—and those of the surrounding East Dalhousie settlements—were on the upswing.

The owners of the new copper mine promised steady work and dividends to all who shelled out hard cash for a piece of the action. People were sceptical at first, but once the company completed the main shaft at ninety feet deep, those same sceptics shook their life savings from their bedrolls and bought shares.

People made plans. Some borrowed on those plans. Young married couples living with their parents dreamed of owning a home of their own, while older couples dreamed of selling them theirs. Farmers imagined bigger barns, teachers imagined better schools, and local politicians imagined longer tenures in public office.

Then calamity struck.

Of course, true Nova Scotians knew that disappointment was coming. They just didn't know how.

There was no earth tremor or mineshaft cave-in, and no global economic crisis that shut operations down. It was a simple matter of embezzlement. The mine manager skipped off with all the money from the sale of stock. He left not a nickel in the till. And when no one stepped forward to reopen and operate the mine, Crossburn and East Dalhousie residents boarded up the entrance and started calling the ninety-foot-deep shaft "the grave of buried hopes."

BOOTLEGGER

Police work isn't what television cracks it up to be. There is more grunt work and door knocking in it than flashes of brilliance. There are also instances of good fortune, and sometimes it is a simple matter of asking the right person the right question.

More than fifty years ago, when the Department of National Defence was building Canadian Forces Base Gagetown in New Brunswick, the area around the base was rife with bootleggers. For nearly a week that winter, a pair of undercover Mounties had gone out patrolling for the worst of those bootleggers without having any luck.

One of the most persistent bootleggers catering to the workmen on the base was a man named Hazen Howland. Hazen, who lived three kilometres from the construction site, was short, bow-legged, and rude. He smoked a short bulldog pipe that twitched in his toothless mouth whenever he got agitated.

That the Mounties always get their man is something of a by-word—well, maybe not always, and in recent years, only sometimes. But now and again they do get their man, by a stroke of luck or a flash of police genius.

One of the undercover Mounties hit on the idea of asking a group of kids if one of them knew where a fellow could get a taste of rum. One lad said, "Sure, I know!" The Mounties invited the youngster to show them where, and the kid led them straight to Hazen Howland's door.

The first one out of the car was the kid, whose name was Douglas. He burst into the farmhouse and yelled out: "These two men want t' buy a pint a' rum. I told them you got lots of it in the cellar."

Hazen Howland just stared at the two men, and twitched the bulldog pipe in his mouth.

The Mounties got their man (and his rum) only because one of them had asked the right question to the right person: Douglas Howland, Hazen's own son.

EMBEZZLEMENT

Fraud and embezzlement have a modern-day ring to them. There is something almost white collar about the sound of those words, a sound associated with sharp pencils scribbling phoney numbers across a general ledger. So it comes as a surprise to read about a case of embezzlement that took place in Nova Scotia nearly two hundred years ago.

In September 1825, Isaac Harpool and his three sons—George, John, and Benjamin—sailed their sloop out from the small settlement at Jeddore, along Nova Scotia's Eastern Shore, and into Halifax Harbour. There, they loaded the vessel with rum, flour, molasses, and nails—goods they intended to sell at the Bay of Chaleur in northeastern New Brunswick. Before setting sail, Isaac visited the office of Messieurs Yeoman and Dolby, and bought insurance on both his boat and the trade goods.

A few days later, word reached Halifax that the Harpool sloop had hit a log not far from its homeport at Jeddore, and sunk.

That brought on an investigation by Yeoman and Dolby, who made inquiries about the Harpool clan, and sailed to the wreck site to confirm that the sloop was on the bottom. Satisfied that all was on the up and up, they paid Isaac Harpool the insurance money.

Then tongues started wagging along the Eastern Shore, and what they wagged about was that Isaac and his sons had pulled a fast one on the insurance brokers. The rumour reached Halifax in the fall of 1825. Yeoman and Dolby, beside themselves to think that they had been duped, charged John Liddell, a police magistrate, to conduct his own investigation.

Liddell sailed to Jeddore to ask Isaac Harpool and his sons a few questions. But the grapevine proved faster than a coastal cutter and, forewarned days before the policeman arrived, the Harpools hightailed it inland, where they hid out for the next several days.

Their mistake was leaving behind their servant, James Maskell. Frightened that Liddell would pin the blame on him, Maskell decided to find John Liddell before Liddell found him. The two knuckled down in a dark corner of a grog shop, and Maskell told Liddell the whole story.

After loading the sloop in Halifax, Maskell and the Harpools had sailed to Jeddore and unloaded everything except a few supplies. Then they set sail for the Bay of Chaleur with a whaleboat in tow. They soon anchored off a large island. Maskell went ashore to fetch two large logs, and floated them ahead of the ship. Apparently Ben Harpool was a deeply religious man, and if the insurance investigators asked him to swear on a Bible that the sloop had struck driftwood, he wanted to be able to do so in good conscience.

Here, Maskell made sure he covered for himself by carefully explaining that he was a servant doing only what he had been ordered to do. He added that George Harpool, the youngest of the brothers, had refused to do his father's dirty work.

Then Maskell lowered his head and told Liddell how the sloop had struck the drifting logs intentionally, and that he himself had gone below and axed out a hole in the bow to scuttle the sloop. Half an hour later, it was on the bottom.

Liddell immediately had a warrant sworn out for the arrest of Isaac Harpool and his three sons on the charge of embezzlement. Then he sailed to Jeddore with an armed guard to enforce the warrant.

Again he arrived too late. Isaac, John, and Benjamin had set sail for the United States in the whaleboat. George Harpool was shackled and transported to Halifax, where he and James Maskell stood trial. They were both acquitted—George for taking no part in the crime, and Maskell for following his master's orders. Both testified on behalf of the other.

As for Isaac, John, and Benjamin, they either ended up adrift in the Gulf of Maine, or down in the Boston States, living off the insurance money they had embezzled.

WAR WITH RUSSIA

On May 11, 1825, Samuel Cunard, the shipping magnate, banged open the door of the *Novascotian* newspaper and entered the crowded office in a damp blast of spring air. Close behind were Enos Collins, Canada's first banker, and William Black, another of Halifax's leading merchants. All three were full of blister and anger. They bullied their way through the composing room, upsetting a galley tray laid out with the following day's edition, knocking the composing stick from the compositor's hand, and scattering lead letters all over the room.

The clatter and commotion roused George Young, the editor, from his private office to confront the great businessmen. But Sam Cunard beat him to the attack.

Cunard held up a copy of a newspaper and demanded to know if this was Young's doing.

The newspaper was the *Saint John Star*. The headline was written in large block letters: "Halifax at War With Russia."

This newspaper had hit the Halifax streets two days before. It passed quickly through the crowd on the waterfront, and among those conducting business at the Exchange Coffee House. The story had turned smiles into frowns, and business banter into anxious murmurs. It reported that Russian troops were sailing for Cuba, to help Spain regain the American colonies it had lost at the close of the Napoleonic War. Great Britain, the story continued, opposed such a move, and ordered the Halifax garrison to go to Havana and intercept the Russian ships. The packet boat carrying news from England was late to arrive in Halifax, and so the Saint John newspaper was Nova Scotia's first intelligence that Great Britain and her colonies were at war.

Soldiers stiffened at this sudden and unexpected end to the long peace. Merchants and shipowners slumped at the prospect of war in the Caribbean and a halt to their lucrative trade with the West Indies.

Despite the lack of official orders from Great Britain, the military prepared for war. They loaded ships with cannons and shot. Behind the city at Camp Hill, the garrison stepped-up their combat drills. Townsfolk, especially young women, walked the streets in sadness at the prospect of the soldiers marching off to war. Worse, prices and stocks in Halifax fell by 5 percent. This caused havoc among local merchants, especially Sam Cunard, Enos Collins, and William Black, whose businesses depended on free trade with the Caribbean.

For two days, Halifax was draped in black crepe—until the afternoon of May 11, when the packet boat from England finally anchored at King's Wharf. Townsfolk crowded the waterfront, eager for news of the war—but there was none. Not a peep from the ship's crew. Not a printed word in the government dispatches.

It had all been a hoax. Someone had printed a phoney copy of the Saint John Star and circulated it throughout Halifax. And that's why Cunard and company barged into the office of the *Novascotian*, demanding to know if George Young was the culprit who had cost them money.

Young did not answer, but stooped to gather the lead type into the galley tray.

Collins pounded his fist on a nearby desk, and challenged, "What kind of editor would print such a falsehood?"

Young retrieved the composing stick and passed it to the compositor, along with the galley tray. "I am sure I do not know, sir," he answered. "But he must be an editor with a great sense of humour."

With that, the three great businessmen turned on their heels and barrelled out of the newspaper office.

Afterward, George Young kept his silence. Though he had not been the prankster, he probably knew who was.

That same headline could have run in the *Novascotian* twenty-five years later—only then it would have been right on the money. By the 1850s, Great Britain was indeed at war with Russia. This was the Crimean War, fought by the British against the Russians in defence of Turkey.

Halifax has an impressive monument to prove it: the Welsford-Parker Monument. It is located just inside a black iron gate at St. Paul's Burying Ground on Barrington Street, and its multiple tiers of sculpted stone could almost overwhelm a visitor. A stone lion stands on top. It honours two Nova Scotia soldiers who died fighting in that senseless, almost forgotten war during the 1850s. They died during the siege of a Russian naval base at Sebastapol on the Crimean Peninsula, storming the barricades in a battle that settled nothing and accomplished even less.

The British fought the war badly from the start. Ill-equipped and ill supplied, more British soldiers died from hunger and disease than from Russian bullets.

But not Major Augustus Frederick Welsford and Captain William Parker. No, they died in the thick of battle.

Major Welsford commanded the Ninety-seventh Regiment, and led the first party to storm the Radan, one of the fortresses guarding Sebastapol. His soldiers carried ladders for climbing the monstrous walls. They were the first to come under the heavy Russian guns; first to charge into the crack and thunder of death; first to shed their blood in a bloodbath. And Welsford was first up the ladders and about to scale the parapet when a cannonball ripped off his head.

Captain Parker was the last to stand on that blood-soaked parapet; the last to cry, "Follow me!", to the dead and dying in the ditch below; the last to raise his rifle to attack, before gunfire riddled his body to pieces. And he was the last to die before the British command called a retreat—the last to die in the last battle of an utterly senseless war.

A few years later, on July 17, 1860, more than two hundred men and women crowded St. Paul's Burying Ground for the dedication of the Welsford-Parker Monument. Bands paraded. Soldiers marched. There was much pomp and circumstance, and dignitaries addressed the public with more bully huff than common sense. They hyped the glory of war and sacrifice in battle, banging their breasts for those who'd given their lives for Queen and Empire—the tens of thousands who never seem to die in vain.

Reverend George Hill recounted the deeds of Major Welsford and Captain Parker. Then the veil fell from the monument to reveal the standing lion, the symbol of British might, standing atop a mass of chocolate-coloured stone. The band struck up "God Save the Queen." Soldiers rattled to attention. Alexander Keith, the grand master of the Masonic Lodge, barked his members into a Masonic salute, and Major-General Charles Trollope fumbled his sword from its scabbard and raised it in a pretentious gesture of loyalty.

Then soldiers and citizens marched from the burying ground, leaving behind George Liang, the builder and sculptor of the monument, to ponder what he had created: A monument whose massive base, bearing the name Welsford-Parker, dwarfs the mighty British lion on top, and seemingly ranks British tribute second to Nova Scotia honour; a monument whose sheer mass testifies to the tragic weight of war.

UNCHRISTIAN CHRISTIANS

The story of some Christian denominations in New Brunswick isn't always as Christian as the word suggests. In 1792, the Church of England and the Congregationalists claimed ownership of the same church, a large structure in Maugerville, on the St. John River.

The Congregationalists had built the church, but the Anglicans claimed ownership because, according to the law at the time, all church property belonged to the Church of England.

The argument turned violent in the fall of that year, when the Anglican faction sold the hay crop around the parsonage to James Taylor, a local merchant. The Congregationalists believed the hay crop belonged to them, and one night, under the leadership of Jeremiah Burpee, they scythed down the crop of hay and hid it in the barn of a fellow Congregationalist.

James Taylor, a bad-tempered man, stormed and raved and threatened the Congregationalists with every punishment imaginable. That night, the Anglicans made up their minds to drive the Congregationalists from the church and parsonage once and for all.

A band of Anglicans surrounded the building and sent a barrage of musket balls through the windows. When one of these hit a beam above the preacher's bed, he and his family abandoned the building to the Anglicans.

For the next few years, the Congregationalists and the Anglicans engaged in a bitter, see-saw battle over the church. It was not until 1820 that Reverend Archibald McCallum, an Anglican, calmed the tempers on both sides. For a while at least, he restored to the Christian churches at Maugerville some semblance of Christian spirit.

PRIVATEERING:
A NOVA SCOTIA BUSINESS

People can only take so much abuse. Sooner or later, they ball their backs and rally, telling their abusers, "enough is enough."

In the 1790s, merchants, ships' captains, sailors, and tradesmen in Liverpool, Nova Scotia, did just that. They'd had it up to their eyeballs with being pillaged and plundered by American privateers.

During the American Revolution, from 1776 to 1783, these privately owned American warships preyed on British shipping along the east coast of North America. To the Americans, any ships flying British colours were fair game for having their decks raked with cannon shot and musket fire. This included Nova Scotia trading vessels. Schooners sailed in and out of Nova Scotia ports at great peril and potentially great financial loss.

In 1783, peace relieved the tension, but that peace was short-lived. By the 1790s, the British were at war with France, and the Americans had taken the French side. Once again, American privateers attacked Nova Scotia trading vessels, as well as communities along Nova Scotia's coast. These privateers became such a menace that they had Liverpool Harbour plugged with anchored shipping. Captains and ship owners in Liverpool were unwilling to take a risk for a boatload of beans, beer, or new-cut timber.

Then one sea captain decided not to take it anymore. This was Joseph Freeman. He and several Liverpool merchants petitioned the provincial government in Halifax for fifteen cannons to fit out their own privateer. Governor John Wentworth and the Duke of Kent agreed.

The Liverpool boys called the new privateer the *Charles Mary Wentworth*, after the governor's sickly son. But there was nothing sickly about this new ship. The day it raised sail out of Liverpool Harbour, in August 1797, it looked every bit as menacing as its American counterparts.

Four months later, the *Charles Mary Wentworth* returned with captured ships of her own. All were loaded to the gunnels with cocoa, cotton, sugar cane, Spanish doubloons, and New England rum.

To celebrate, Joseph Freeman threw a party at Mrs. West's tavern. Most of the town showed up. Hundreds of glasses were raised to the *Charles Mary Wentworth*. There was a lot of backslapping and hand pumping. Liverpool merchants felt it in their bones that the ship's privateering success augured the start of something big—and it sure did!

The *Charles Mary Wentworth* made a dozen more successful privateering ventures, and launched Liverpool into a growing industry—one that cut a fine line between legitimate military action and government-authorized piracy.

The British Crown began issuing letters of marques to Nova Scotia ships like it was going out of style. A letter of marque was an open licence for a Nova Scotia ship to prey on all ships considered enemies to the British Crown. It was now open season on American, French, and Spanish ships, and Nova Scotian shipowners were quick to take advantage of it.

On August 12, 1800, this ad appeared in a Nova Scotia newspaper: "All Gentlemen volunteers, Seamen, and able bodied landsmen, who wish to acquire riches and honour are invited to repair on board the *Rover* Privateer Ship of War now laying in Halifax Harbour; bound on a cruise to the southward for four months against the French, and all His Majesty's Enemies, and then to return to this harbour."

The *Rover* had been built and fitted for war. It mounted fourteen cannons, and carried a crew of fifty-five men, boys, and officers. Alex Godfrey was the captain.

On September 10, 1800, Captain Godfrey sighted and attacked a Spanish merchant schooner off the coast of Venezuela. Suddenly, Godfrey sighted three gunboats and a warship flying Spanish colours, all sailing full speed to assist the crippled schooner. As the Spanish ships approached, the warship fired her forward guns, and the *Rover* made a run for open water.

The Spanish closed in, and drew within pistol range. The gunboats drew alongside the *Rover*, with the warship behind them. Still Captain Alex Godfrey remained calm—even as the Spanish crews clung to Rover's gunnels and prepared to board his ship.

Barely fifteen yards separated the gunboats from the *Rover*, when Captain Godfrey ordered his Nova Scotian crew to ply the oars on the port side. This swung the *Rover* broadside to the warship. On Godfrey's command, seven cannons fired together, sounding like one and raking the Spanish warship from bow to stern. In the next moment, the *Rover*'s crew swivelled their cannons on the gunboats, and poured out volley after volley.

Just as quickly, and working like madmen, the *Rover*'s crew swung the heavy guns back toward the warship. They fired chain shot into the warship's rigging and spars, bringing down masts, ropes, and canvas on top of the Spanish crew. Then they turned back for another round on the gunboats, and then another on the warship. They kept swivelling and firing until they crippled the gunboats and sent them limping back out to sea. Finally, the crew of the *Rover* poured over the side of the Spanish warship *Santa Ritta* and captured her.

In a matter of minutes, and with a show of raw courage, Godfrey and his crew had turned the tables on the attacking Spanish ships. And they had done so without losing a single man.

The return voyage to Halifax was one of triumph for Godfrey and his crew. Godfrey had held true to the promise in his newspaper advertisement, which had called for volunteers "who wish to acquire riches and honour...on board the *Rover* Privateer Ship of War."

TRADING WITH THE ENEMY

For a fair chunk of the eighteenth century, France and England were either at war with each other or pretending to be. And that meant their North American colonies squabbled with each other as well. England and France demanded their colonies have no truck with the enemy, but on that score, the English were much more insistent than the French. Many Nova Scotia and New England merchants plied a lucrative trade with the French in Quebec and in the French-controlled areas of Acadie (Nova Scotia). English warships patrolled the Gulf of Maine and the Bay of Fundy trying to stop the smuggling. Like the interdiction efforts against drug smuggling today, only occasionally did they get lucky.

The *Nancy-Sally*, a Nova Scotia coastal schooner, flew British colours one day and French the next. The *Nancy-Sally* was a smuggler's ship, and in 1754, it signalled its allegiance according to the side it was trading with.

Her captain was John Hovey, a slippery devil who ran a smuggler's game that played both sides—French and British—between Nova Scotia and the New England colonies. His principal ports of call were Halifax, Fortress Louisburg, Annapolis Royal, Beausejour, and Boston.

Captain Hovey had a seven-man crew: Benjamin Street, Samuel Thornton, John Pastree, John Neale, Sam Wheland, Jean Baptiste Porlieu, and his own brother, Joseph Hovey.

In early July 1754, Captain McKenzie of His Majesty's warship *Vulture* spotted the *Nancy-Sally* sailing into the Bay of Fundy under British colours. A few days later, McKenzie saw the same schooner on its return and flying a French flag. That was reason enough for Captain McKenzie to raise sail and give chase.

According to McKenzie's testimony in Vice-Admiralty court, John Hovey and his crew had been trading with the enemy at Beausejour. As the *Vulture* closed on the *Nancy-Sally* and fired a warning shot across her bow, Hovey and his crew made a run for it into Musquash Cove. The *Vulture* followed, and launched a barge with an eight-man boarding crew. And that's when it all got ugly.

As the barge drew alongside the *Nancy-Sally*, Samuel Thornton loaded the schooner's swivel gun, and John Pastree did the same with the musketoon (an eighteenth-century shotgun). Both fired at the *Vulture*'s boarding party once. The double blast opened up Isaac Jolly's stomach and peppered apart Tom McDermot's head.

The rest of the British boarding party drew their cutlasses and fought the smugglers into submission.

Once the smugglers had been subdued, Captain McKenzie boarded and searched their ship. Below deck, he found contraband furs, sheep, cattle, and sundry other goods. Neale, Wheyland, and Joseph Hovey were caught hiding among the cargo. Captain John Hovey was in his cabin, doubled over with stomach cramps—or so he claimed.

At the smugglers' murder trial before Chief Justice Jonathan Belcher in Halifax, there was a lot of finger pointing and desperate denials that they had anything to do with murdering two sailors off the HMS *Vulture*. Ben Street admitted to being on deck, but denied helping with the swivel gun or firing the musketoon. John Pastree claimed much the same thing. He said he had loaded the gun, but had not fired it.

Porlieu said he was a passenger heading for Annapolis Royal, and had nothing to do with the smuggling or the fight against the *Vulture*'s crew. And those caught hiding among the cargo testified that they had scrambled below deck at the first signs of trouble, and had taken no part in the gunplay or sword-fighting.

Captain McKenzie was unable to say for sure which of those caught on deck had done the shooting, other than to point an accusing finger at Samuel Thornton, who had been captured standing beside the swivel gun.

Thornton admitted to using the firebrand that touched off the swivel gun, but clung to the excuse that he had done so under his captain's orders and in self-defence. He had believed the boarding party were pirates.

How Thornton could have mistaken a British warship flying British colours for a pirate ship challenges one's gullibility—but it may have been possible. At least, it raised enough doubt for Chief Justice Belcher to acquit them all. It's quite possible he did so on the grounds of the confusing, conflicting, and insufficient evidence, but more probably he spared them the gallows because these able-bodied sailors could better serve His Majesty as impressed seamen in the stinking bowels of a British warship.

And that's where Thornton, Pashtree, and Street found themselves—on board the *Vulture*, serving alongside hardened, weathered sailors who bore them a grudge for the murder of their mates.

John Neale, Sam Wheyland, Jean Baptiste Porlieu, and Joseph Hovey walked out of Belcher's courtroom free and clear, acquitted of all charges and with no obligation to serve in His Majesty's navy.

Captain John Hovey never went to trial. As captain of the *Nancy–Sally*, he knew it was more than likely that the full weight of the law would land on his head. And so a few days before the trial, he escaped jail and—despite a reward of twenty pounds for his capture—managed to flee Nova Scotia to places unknown.

SCAMPS

AND

SCOUNDRELS

MACINTYRE'S MILL

On the south side of the Annapolis River in Lawrencetown, Nova Scotia, and beside the Highway 1 where it crosses a small brook, there used to be an old water-powered mill. This was MacIntyre's Mill, where at one time, just about every farmer in the surrounding countryside brought his wool for carding.

Springtime was sheep-shearing time. Once the raw fleece was washed and dried, there were generally long lineups of farmers waiting their turn at MacIntyre's mill.

John MacIntyre was a stern and cranky old man who spoke little and scowled much. He had no friends and lived alone. That was about as much as anyone knew about John MacIntyre—except that he'd made a fortune with that mill, spent little of it, and kept his gold hidden somewhere on the property.

One spring morning in 1890, MacIntyre's neighbours smelled smoke coming from the carding mill. When they arrived, they found the mill burned to the ground and MacIntyre face down in the mud beside the brook. He was dead. The back of his head had been caved by a hand-sized rock that lay on the ground beside his body.

No one knew who killed John MacIntyre, or whether the killer found MacIntyre's hoard of gold. For decades afterwards, many believed that MacIntyre's money still lay buried somewhere beside that brook in Lawrencetown.

THE MURDER OF
SADIE MCAULEY

On the morning of August 4, 1921, nine-year-old Sadie McAuley from north end Saint John went raspberry picking with eleven-year-old Harriet Lavigne. When Harriet tired of berry picking and called to Sadie that she was going home, there was no reply.

All that day, Sadie's family and friends searched the steep bank that led down to the waters of Marble Cove, but with no luck. The next day, police and volunteers combed the area, but still had no luck.

A week later, James Kimball went berry picking along the slope at Marble Cove, and saw the decomposing body of Sadie McAuley under a large, flat rock. Police investigated and determined Sadie had been murdered. The local newspaper offered a five-hundred-dollar reward for her killer. Then the city doubled the reward—and that brought results.

Walter Humphrey, an unsavoury Saint John character, came forward. He said he'd had a fight with a black man named John Paris the night before the murder. Then another man came forward and said he had rowed John Paris to the Douglas Avenue area, where Sadie had been killed.

When asked how he learned of the killing, Humphrey said he read of it in the *Saint John Standard* on August 3—but the newspaper had had mechanical troubles, and wasn't published that day. Still, no one questioned Humphrey's story closely. The public outcry was powerful, and the police were under tremendous pressure. They desperately needed a guilty party.

And John Paris was an ideal candidate: he was from Truro, Nova Scotia, lived in a rough section of Saint John, had a few prior brushes with the law, was poor and illiterate—and he was a black man. The Saint John police went to Truro, where Paris had gone, and brought him back to Saint John. They arraigned him, gave him a preliminary hearing, and charged him with Sadie MacAuley's murder.

Paris's first two trials ended with hung juries. There was just not enough evidence to convict. Besides, Walter Humphrey—a criminal himself—was an unreliable witness. By the fifth trial, Chief Justice H. A. McKewan had had enough. He set a one-thousand-dollar bail bond, lest another trial should be held, and told Paris to go home to Truro.

Saint John citizens were outraged. They wanted Paris convicted.

Weeks later, a Saint John cop was in Truro working another case. He was thumbing through the police court records when he noticed that on the day Sadie McAuley was brutally murdered in Saint John, John Paris was in the Truro jail, accused of stealing gasoline.

Perhaps Paris did steal two gallons of gas in Truro; but he did not kill Sadie McAuley in Saint John. And to this day no one knows who did.

COLONEL DAVID FANNING

The prisoner's leg irons grumbled as he rose to hear the bailiff read the charge:

"Colonel David Fanning, Esquire, of Hamstead in the County of Queens, New Brunswick, you are hereby arraigned before this court on the following true bill of indictment. That on September 27, 1800, you did make an assault on the body of Sarah London of Wickham, and against her will did feloniously ravish and carnally know and commit other wrongs to the said Sarah London, to the great damage of the peace of our Lord the King, His Crown, and His dignity. How do you answer?"

The small, wood-framed courthouse in Burton, New Brunswick, creaked under the weight of so many spectators craning forward at once. Even the tribunal of judges—James Peters, Samuel Dickinson, and Chief Justice George Ludlow—straightened for the prisoner's response. They expected to hear a tongue-lashing from such a hot-tempered man.

Colonel Fanning straightened his nail of a body. His thin face lengthened. "Not guilty!" he said, and the red bandana he wore to hide the honeycomb of scabby blotches on the top of his head slipped down to his shoulder, revealing the skull of a hard-boned man as raw and rugged as his reputation.

Colonel David Fanning was the elected member of the New Brunswick House of Assembly from Queens County. He owned a gristmill and a sawmill, as well as thousands of acres of land on a small stream in Hampstead that still bears his name. Fanning was wealthy, a gentleman and a war hero. He had earned his reputation as a hard-fighting, blood-running soldier while he fought in the Carolina backcountry during the American Revolution.

During the Revolution, the fighting in the Carolinas was scrappier, more individually violent, and more terrifying than in the other colonies. It had more in common with a blood feud than a war. On both sides of the conflict, personal or family vengeance had motivated the call to arms more than any deeply felt belief in political principles. The argument over British rule only widened the cracks between this family and that, and between one clan of settlers and another.

Before the outbreak of the American Revolution, Fanning had been something of a loner. He ran a trade between Fort Ninety-Six in backcountry South Carolina and the Catawba and Cherokee tribes that trapped and hunted in the foothills of the Blue Ridge Mountains. The only politics he had ever cared about were the politics that kept his customers at peace and him in business. So in Ninety Six, when the tavern talk got around to loud shouts for American independence, Fanning found himself siding with those who shouted back in favour of British rule. He just wanted things to remain as they had always been. He wanted to keep trading, and said so. But what he said was not what the local Committee of Public Safety, the local gang of rebel thugs, wanted to hear. So the committee tracked him down, put him in jail, and threatened that if Fanning did not side with the cause of independence, they would hang him the same way they had hanged two other Loyalists the day before.

The following night, Fanning escaped, and later joined an outfit of Loyalists under Patrick and William ("Bloody Bill")

Cunningham. As far as the Cunningham brothers were concerned, there were no enemies on their side of the musket. Within months, the Cunningham gang had swelled to a mix of well-intentioned friends of the king, outlaws on the run, and thugs. A few fought for law and government, but most of them raided and killed for some personal grudge, for the loot they pillaged, for the pure joy of fighting.

On January 2, 1776, the Cunningham gang of Loyalists suffered defeat by the Revolutionaries in a close-up, smoke-faced fight at the Great Cane Break, a mosquito-driven swamp between the Broad and Saluda Rivers. A few months later, they suffered a more crippling defeat at Kings Mountain, where they ran head-on into a sizable army of American Revolutionaries. The Loyalists scattered and took to the hills or the swamps. Some sought cover in the North Carolina backcountry.

Fanning was among a dozen men left scavenging to stay alive in the thick underbrush, all mud-soaked and bloody, festering with sores and burning with fever. They found refuge in Cross Creek, North Carolina, a jut of swampland near the Pee Dee River. There among the reeds and cattails, pestered by the canopy squawk of jays and crows, tortured by the bites of mosquitoes, and threatened by the quiet slither of water moccasins, they hunkered down in sickness and silence—until one of their own boiled down his anger and steamed his temper. That man furiously pulled aside the heavy skin of fear that covered these Loyalists; he bolstered their backbones with his own marrow and ran their bad blood into a dark pool of vengeance. That man was David Fanning.

What moved Fanning from follower to leader, from a self-reliant loner to the snarl- and hate-driven heart of a gang of terrorists, was war. War not only brings out the worst in men from their cubbies of contempt, it also makes heroes of those with a mood for wild rage and a disregard for death.

By 1780, Fanning's small band of guerrilla fighters terrorized the North Carolina countryside. "Swamp fighting" was what they called their style of steamy and twisted back and forth ambush and close-up killing, and their hit-and-run raids on farms, villages, supply lines, and small patrols of Revolutionary cavalry.

The North Carolina Loyalists welcomed Fanning as an avenging angel against the outlaw Revolutionaries and their vigilante gangs called "Committees of Public Safety." The Loyalists rallied around him, and followed his charge across Wade, Montgomery, and Randolph Counties.

While the Loyalists praised David Fanning, the Revolutionaries and the Sons of Liberty—the rebels against British law and government—cursed him. They hated Fanning, feared him, and shivered at the sound of his name. They called him a terrorist, a tartar, a will-o'-the-wisp criminal who burned and pillaged and committed cold-blooded murder.

In 1780, when the British turned the theatre of war from the northern colonies to the south, they favoured Fanning with an officer's commission for his relentless aggression against the king's enemies. It was a commission of convenience, an easy recognition for the British to give to one of the few willing and able to fight in a war that had soured against them.

Fanning's reputation grew—and with it, the size of his army. By 1781, they numbered more than a thousand men. Several times he backed down North Carolina State Militia units that were twice the size of his own force, and once he fought off a contingent of the American Continental Army. Fanning's greatest achievement came in the summer of 1781, when he out-manoeuvred a combined army of state militia and Continental soldiers, marched into the state capitol at Hillsborough, and captured the North Carolina General Assembly and the governor, Thomas Burke.

The war, however, soon turned against him. No sooner did the British wave the white flag at Yorktown, Virginia, in the fall of 1781 than the North Carolina Revolutionaries narrowed their sights on a single target: David Fanning. Regiments of American Continentals and state militia went "Tory hunting." They turned every stone in their hunt for Fanning, and avenged their failures by raiding Tory farms, burning what they couldn't steal, and sometimes killing anyone they found at home.

Fanning retaliated, torch for torch and blood for blood. He fought for more than a year after the truce. He protected those Loyalists who could not protect themselves, and herded them to the safety of British lines on the coast.

In these last days, Fanning took a wife, Sarah Carr. A Justice of the Peace married them at the Carr family home near Cross Creek, North Carolina. No sooner had the couple said their vows than a Revolutionary patrol attacked. Fanning and Sarah made for the horses and the woods. Fanning's best man, Bill Hooker, wasn't so lucky. Hooker burst from the house to a hail of musket fire, and went down in the mud just outside the door.

Fanning and Sarah honeymooned on the run. Sarah was eighteen, and more spice than sugar, more frightened than in love. Fanning sent her to live among the Loyalist refugees at Charleston. Then, with a musket across his lap and dragoon pistols in his belt, as well as a short sword and a hunting knife, Fanning fought on—if for no other reason than the hate of it. He kept fighting until his eyes were too teary to take aim and his arms too heavy to strike.

In 1783, Fanning fled North Carolina for Charleston, and from Charleston to Florida. From there, he and his family—he and Sarah now had a son—made their way to Saint John, New Brunswick, and then upriver to the overhang of hills where the river splits around Spoon Island and pools at Hampstead.

For all the quiet of the countryside and the steady peace of the river, in Fanning's mind, the war was still too close, the memories too vivid, and the killing too raw to be forgiven.

At first, the New Brunswick Loyalists welcomed Fanning as something of a war hero who had fought savagely for king and government, and who had put his life on the line in defence of the Carolina Loyalists and their families. By 1800, however, the flame of Fanning's welcome had burned down to cold ash. The quick temper, rage, and brutality that had made him a ferocious fighter during the war made him a miserable, mean-spirited, bad-tempered son of a bitch after it. Fanning became one of the most disliked men living along the St. John River. His neighbours easily believed the worst of him. They thought Fanning capable of any crime laid against him, including the charge he now faced: rape.

After Fanning's plea, Chief Justice George Ludlow gavelled the court to silence. Thomas Hansford, the Crown prosecutor, called his first witness: John Golding.

John Golding—a weedy man who had starched his collar and blackened his boots for the occasion—took the witness stand. Golding was the local magistrate, the Justice of the Peace. He held a grudge against Fanning, and everyone in the courthouse knew it. For the past several years, Golding and Fanning had been at each other's throats over politics—local politics, the kind that benefit one neighbour over another. Fanning held the higher office, but Golding delivered the political plums.

Fanning had opposed Golding's appointment as Justice of the Peace on the grounds that Golding was illiterate and incompetent. He claimed Golding's appointment was the latest example of government patronage. And it was.

Patronage was the heart and soul of colonial government in New Brunswick—and Fanning was as much a part of this political system as anyone. He was not against patronage. He just wanted to be the man holding the bowl and passing out the fruit.

After Golding took office, Fanning bent every which way to get him removed, and Golding hated Fanning for it. He once swore at Gutherie's Tavern that he would get even with David Fanning.

Everyone in court also knew what Golding was about to say. There were few secrets among the Loyalist settlers of Wickham and Hampstead. So on September 27, 1800, when Sarah London stopped at Mary Brown's house and then, three hours later, at Desire Clark's, telling them how Colonel Fanning had "used her ill" and that she was on her way to complain to the Justice of the Peace, the river rippled and the eel grass bent in the steady breeze of so much conversation.

John Golding further fanned the gossip by dropping a word or two of his own about what Sarah London had told him:

> ...that on the 27 September she went to pay a visit to the family of David Fanning...and when she came to the door, which was two half doors with the upper half open, she saw Colonel Fanning lying on his bed. She asked where his wife and two daughters was. Colonel Fanning got off his bed and laid violent hands on her arm and dragged her into his house and threw her onto his bed. Sarah London began to cry and told him to let her go or she would tell her father. Fanning replied that he did not care for that. Fanning pulled up her petticoats and unbuttoned his breeches and used his utmost efforts to have carnal knowledge of her body. She was crying and struggling to rescue herself from him. He put his hands across her mouth and tried to suffocate her. With great difficulty she got clear from him.

Fanning publicly denied all the backyard talk. He said Sarah London had come knocking after his wife and daughter had gone to market. He claimed she had wanted to borrow a book—something about Cook's voyages to the new world. When Fanning told her he did not have this book, she shrugged and said Fanning had something else she wanted. She lay on the bed, and Fanning lifted her petticoats. Her under bodice was as filthy as a muckheap, he claimed, and the stink was strong enough to make him choke. He told her to get out, and when she refused, he threw her out. That was all that happened, Fanning said. Nothing more.

But his outhouse words to Sarah London about her cleanliness and character riled the girl into having something to say herself. She told her friends, her parents, and thus most of those living on the lower St. John River, that on that harvest morning, with the Fanning women off to market, the colonel had dragged her into the house, thrown her on the daybed, held a sword at her throat, and "had his way."

Those words, "had his way"—formally stated before the Justice of the Peace three days after her first declaration that the colonel had "used her ill"—changed the charge against David Fanning from simple assault to rape. With those words, Sarah London had upped the ante.

The time lag of three days was the backbone of Fanning's defence. According to *Blackstone's Commentaries* on the evidence for rape:

...if the victim be of evil fame and stands unsupported by others, if she concealed the injury for any length of time after she had opportunity to complain, if the place where the act alleged to be committed was where it was possible she might have been heard and she made no outcry, these and the like circumstances carry a strong but not conclusive presumption that her testimony is false and feigned.

On all three counts, the Crown's case against Fanning was weak. Sarah London was well known to be "bold in her manners." She had made no outcry—none that her own brother, who had ferried her to Fanning's house and docked nearby, could hear. And she had gone berry picking for three hours immediately after the supposed assault, and waited three days to lay the charge of rape.

With John Golding on the witness stand, the prosecution reminded the tribunal of judges and the jury of Fanning's rough reputation. Golding told the court that Fanning had recently been charged with assault twice: once for pushing Elizabeth Mullen into the mud because he wanted to be first on a boardwalk across the mire, and a second time for punching Adrian Pitch, who had scolded Fanning for what he had done to Liz Mullen. The assault on Liz Mullen had cost Fanning five pounds, and the one on Adrian Pitch had cost him five pounds more.

Golding then testified that Sarah London had barged into his office, accusing Colonel Fanning of having his way with her. Golding said he thought she meant Fanning had knocked her about, the way he had done with others. When she returned three days later to say Fanning had in fact raped her, Golding changed the charge against Fanning from assault to rape.

When she took the witness stand, Sarah London confirmed what the river folk had already heard: The pole barge that took her to Fanning's house. The colonel lying on the daybed. His shirt undone, stockings rolled to the ankles, and breeches unbuttoned to the waist. That he was pleased with her visit, and pleased to show himself to her. That he begged her to lie with him and she refused, saying she "don't run goods for rusty guts." Then the sword at her throat. Colonel Fanning's face a wrinkle of meanness as he forced her to the daybed. Forced up her petticoats. Forced her to let him have his way.

But under cross-examination, her testimony bent like a barge pole pushing against the current. When asked by Thomas Wetmore, Fanning's defence attorney, to describe the sword, London couldn't. (Later in the trial, Wetmore called Sheriff Robert Boyle to the stand, and Boyle testified that he had found Fanning's sword in a garret, covered with an inch of dust.)

Then Wetmore pressed London about picking blueberries with Mary Brown immediately after the supposed rape. Sarah explained that her mind had been lathered from the experience, and that she had needed time to compose herself before going to the Justice of the Peace. Wetmore then asked if that was why she also stopped at Desire Clark's house to have tea.

Sam Leydecker later testified that he was anchored off Spoon Island, about two chains (132 feet) away from Fanning's house. He had been handlining for pickerel in the eelgrass. Leydecker said he saw Sarah London run out the front door of Fanning's house and head for the river like she had a belly full of wasps. Her hair was wild, her skirts were flapping, and Colonel Fanning was chasing close behind. Leydecker said he heard her holler something about the colonel hanging for what he had done. The Crown made

Leydecker repeat what he had heard, made him say the words slowly so the jury could make no mistake: Sarah London had hollered that Fanning was a blackleg bastard, and that he would hang for what he had done.

Thomas Wetmore asked Leydecker only two questions under cross-examination.

First, he asked how Leydecker had been injured in the Battle for Harlem Heights during the American Revolution. Leydecker answered that his musket had exploded while firing, and that the blast still rang in his right ear, making him deaf on that side.

Second, Wetmore asked how much money Leydecker owed Colonel Fanning. Leydecker lowered his head, and said that he was in deep to Fanning for a sizable sum: twenty-two pounds and six shillings.

In Fanning's defence, Thomas Wetmore called Mary Brown, Desire Clark, and Sarah Worden to the stand. All three testified that, only hours after her encounter at Fanning's, Sarah London had not been the least bit agitated when she stopped at their houses to respectively pick blueberries, take tea, and walk by the river. They agreed that London had not said a word about rape. Instead, she had bragged that although Fanning had used her ill, she had outrun him, and that she was not afraid of him because he was old and slow.

John London, the girl's brother, testified that he had landed Sarah on the dock at Fanning's house, and then dropped downriver and tied his barge at the mill landing. He said he was well within earshot of Fanning's house, and had heard nothing.

Throughout the trial, Fanning remained calm. He sat coldly in a straight-backed chair and listened. He itched to answer the accusations and the lies, and his lips trembled for the chance to speak his mind in open court. Twice his face pruned with anger to hear the Crown prosecutor besmirch his honour as a gentleman. And once his belly knotted as the Crown belittled his reputation as a soldier. Still, Fanning held himself as though he were in ambush in a Carolina swamp, glaring through the underbrush.

War doesn't just come and go for a soldier who has served in the thick of it. It isn't a blast of wind that bends the trees and then passes. War is more like a long, cold night that shivers the blood and makes it need warming. It is a kind of smoke that sticks in the lungs and sours the belly. There is always the stink of the past that keeps the mind grinding down the edges of another death, another killing. There's always a shudder and a twist, a caught breath that turns time inside out and makes every moment of memory run hot. In a soldier's mind, war is forever.

Fanning had written a narrative of his swamp-fighting days in North Carolina. He wrote the truth about the blood-for-blood killing: the smoke-black burn, the scurry and hunt, the hard swallow, and the stench of a friend's corpse. He wrote with pride and without regret. He wrote coldly, like a man who had long ago snuffed the urge to wince. He wrote like this:

"I came to a house where a Rebel wedding was taking place. There being but five of us, we immediately surrounded the house. Three of my men went into the house and drove them all out one by one. I caused them all to stand in a row to examine them, to see if I knew any of them that were bad men. I found one—William Doody. I then having my pistols in my hands discharged them both at his breast with which he fell dead."

Thomas Hansford submitted the colonel's narrative as evidence for the Crown. He drew attention to several passages, particularly this one: "I then came to Captain John Bryan's house, a Rebel Officer who had killed many Tories. I told him if he would come out of the house I would give a parole, which he refused. With that, I immediately ordered the house to be set on fire."

The prosecution turned Fanning's words against him. Hansford suggested that if Colonel Fanning could execute William Doody in cold blood, if he could set fire to John Bryan's house with Bryan and his family inside and shoot Bryan down as he and his family ran from the burning building, then Fanning was quite capable of raping Sarah London.

The jury retired for less than half an hour. When they returned, William Peters, the foreman, read the verdict: "We the jury find the accused, Colonel David Fanning of Hampstead in the County of Queens, guilty of rape and other crimes and conduct."

Fanning slumped at the verdict, then shook as Chief Justice George Ludlow donned a black cap and pronounced that Fanning was to be "taken from the Bar to the place of imprisonment, and, on Friday, 17 October, 1800, to be taken to the place of execution and there to be hanged by the neck until he is dead, dead, dead."

Fanning lost his grip on the man he once was, the man who could chew his fear into a cud of courage and look down a muzzle without a flinch. The shadow of his past seemed to slip to the floor as the colonel choked on the judge's words—that he had been found "guilty of rape and other crimes and conduct."

Those who had been eager to watch Fanning fight on their side during the war, who had been so thankful for the rebel blood he spilled, were now every bit as eager and thankful to watch him hang. And for what? For rape? On that charge, the evidence did not substantiate a conviction. No, Fanning was found guilty for "other crimes and conduct": for being a man out of place and out of time, a soldier who had outlived the fighting, a war hero whose wild rage and disregard for death ran against the current of a community at peace. The New Brunswick government had tried him for rape, but convicted him of murder during a war in which they had all shared—as though what each of them had done during wartime was not part of who and what they had become.

On the day before Fanning's execution, Thomas Wetmore entered his dank, piss-smelling jail cell and read this document to him:

> To Our Justices of the Supreme Court of Judicature for the Province of New Brunswick, Our Justices of the Peace, Sheriffs, and other Officers of Justice in the said Province and to all our loving subjects—Whereas our Court of Oyer and Terminer held at Gagetown in and for Queens County on Tuesday the thirtieth day of September last that David Fanning, Esquire was indicted and on due trial found guilty and received sentence of Death for the Crime of Rape upon one Sarah London. Now know ye that for divers good causes we do adjudge the said David Fanning a

fit object of our Mercy and we do of our special grace and mercy pardon the said David Fanning from all pains and penalties incurred by the conviction and sentence aforesaid upon the express condition that he the said David Fanning do leave our said Province of New Brunswick on or before the fifteenth day of November next and be not again found within the same.

Thomas Carleton, Governor

Fanning knotted his red bandana on his head, removed his coat from a peg, and followed Wetmore from the jailhouse. The carpenters were still hammering at the gallows.

Fanning and his family travelled to Saint John, where they caught a boat for Digby, Nova Scotia. There Fanning lived out the rest of his days. So long as he was physically able, he eked out a living as a pony express rider between Digby and Kentville. He died of apoplexy on March 14, 1825.

ELIZABETH WATSON

On March 18, 1778, in Halifax, Nova Scotia, Elizabeth Watson—a slave to Elias Marshall—appeared before a Justice of the Peace as a swollen heap of raw, battered flesh. Her open wounds festered with infection. Her voice was feeble.

She told the Justice of the Peace, and later a trial judge, that eight days after Elias Marshall had bought her from William Proud, she revealed that she was pregnant and near to term. Elizabeth carried small, and under multiple layers of clothing, her pregnancy had been well hidden. Marshall's wife hadn't even noticed.

Marshall blew his stack. A pregnant slave was not what he had bargained for. He clipped Elizabeth with a backhand that stunned her, then fetched a thick leather strap, stripped her naked, and laid a beating on her so brutal that her legs buckled and she collapsed to the floor.

The beating must have sent Elizabeth into labour, because later that night, she begged Marshall to get a midwife to help her deliver. Marshall flew into another rage and beat her again—this time more viciously than before, and not with a strap, but with a billet of wood. Marshall then turned her out to the stable to deliver the child on her own.

The following day, Elizabeth was too weak from the beating and from childbirth to rise off the straw in the stable and provide her master with a full day's work. She also complained of being cold. Marshall listened to her complaint, then called another servant to the stable and ordered the servant to fetch cold water and snow. When the servant returned, Marshall doused Elizabeth with the cold water. Then he packed her shivering body in the snow.

That night, after the household had fallen asleep, Elizabeth bundled up her newborn child and ran away. But with a baby on her hip and her legs wobbly from exhaustion, she hardly made it to the end of the street. Marshall found her and dragged her back to his cellar. There, he tied her hands and legs to a beam and beat her for nearly one hour. He did the same at noon, and again that night.

Elizabeth could not lie down, but had to rest on her hands and knees. She was close to death and could barely nurse her baby.

Sensing that he was about to lose his investment, Marshall sent for Dr. Phillips to examine the slave girl. Dr. Phillips determined that she was beyond hope. That set Marshall off into a cursing fit. His tongue became a red rag of abuse and invective for Elizabeth Watson, Dr. Phillips, and William Proud—the man who had sold him the pregnant slave girl in the first place.

Marshall sought a second opinion from Dr. Fletcher, who offered a more promising prognosis: a few days of rest and healthy food, and Elizabeth would be back on her feet and able to carry out her chores.

Chores were not what roused Elizabeth's spirit to regain her health—vengeance was. No sooner was Elizabeth able to stand and walk than she bee-lined for the Justice of the Peace, and charged Elias Marshall with assault and William Proud with imprisonment. At the trial, Elizabeth claimed she had been a free woman who was scooped up and made a slave when the British and the Loyalists retreated from Boston to Halifax after the Battle of Bunker Hill.

William Proud said otherwise. He produced a bill of sale from George Lodell of Boston for one slave named "Phyllis," and claimed this was the same slave now calling herself Elizabeth Watson. Proud also showed the court his paperwork for selling the same slave girl to Elias Marshall.

Elizabeth had no paperwork to support her status as a free woman. And she had only own her word that she was not the slave woman named Phyllis recorded in the bill of sale. The issue boiled down to the word of a black woman against that of a white man. The court ruled in favour of William Proud.

As for Elias Marshall and the charge of assault, since the court had ruled that Elizabeth Watson was a slave girl named Phyllis and Marshall's rightful property—as per his bill of sale from William Proud—the charge against him was dropped.

DIRTY MARY MCGUIRE

Mary McGuire was a puny, filthy, raggedly dressed woman whose breath smelled like a gin shop. She was a back-alley wench with an outhouse for a mouth, a mashed-in nose, and a face full of scars and bruises from more than one fist that had tried to shut her up. She had been born to poverty in Halifax, and over the past thirty-four years, her luck had gone from bad to worse.

On March 30, 1825, for the nineteenth time in as many years, Dirty Mary McGuire appeared in court on a charge of theft. This time, she had swiped two shirts from the backroom of a boarding house, and made no bones about having done it. Stealing was Mary's ticket back into the workhouse, where she did not have to worry about a place to sleep or where her next meal was coming from.

In a voice that sounded like a rusted wagon wheel, Dirty Mary McGuire told the court that she was guilty of whatever the Crown wanted to charge her with. As the *Novascotian* newspaper reported, Mary McGuire called the workhouse her home, and said that being on the outside was "to be damned to hell."

HALIFAX'S FIRST MURDER

Life was hard for Halifax's first settlers. It was also cruel, and often violent. Booze helped numb the mind to the hardness of the times, and during that first winter in 1749, it also helped chase the chill from the bones of those hunkered down in makeshift huts and cabins. By the time April's sun sucked the frost from the earth, a good many Halifax settlers had eagerly traded their valuables for the warm bliss of rum. Silver spoons bought a keg, and brass buckles a jug, and breeches, hose, and whalebone buttons bought a gallon, a quart, and a gill, respectively.

Booze dulled the mind and fired the emotions, and helped create the circumstances for violent times. Halifax's first murder resulted from a night and day of heavy drinking.

On August 21, 1749, a month after the transport ships had dropped anchor in Halifax Harbour, Abram Goodside, a sailor and a bull of a man, awoke from a drunken sleep to find himself among the tents pitched on the beach. Peter Carteel, a settler, was standing over him and threatening him with a knife

Carteel called Goodside a stinking jack-tar because of an unfinished, drunken argument they'd had the night before. Goodside stared hard at the knife, then backed off.

At five o'clock that afternoon, Goodside went to Carteel's tent. He had spent the day fuelling his anger with rum. He challenged the settler to come out of the tent and face him.

Fearful for his life, and drunk himself, Carteel drew a knife from his boot, threw open the tent flap, and lunged at Abram Goodside. The strong blow lifted Goodside up on his toes. He groaned once as the knife went straight into his heart, then collapsed into Carteel's arms. As Carteel pushed him away and yanked out the knife, Goodside went down on the beach in a spray of blood.

Halifax was but a town of tents clinging to a mud-covered hillside, a settlement without a jail or a courthouse. Carteel was tried in the ordnance tent, among barrels of flour and pickled pork.

The provost marshal, William Foy, led the accused into the tent, and the bailiff read the charge: "That Peter Carteel, not having the fear of God before his eyes but being moved and seduced by the instigation of the devil did draw his knife and stab to death Abram Goodside."

Carteel admitted to drawing the knife after Goodside challenged him. But he said he did not stab him, and claimed that Goodside, being drunk, fell on the knife during the scuffle. Carteel said he then ran away, in fear of being murdered by those who chased him.

Three witnesses appeared for the Crown: George Musgrove, Peter Masters, and Roger Sowdow, a town constable. Sowdow testified that earlier in the day, the two men had had a quarrel, and that Carteel had drawn a knife and threatened Goodside. Then Masters and Musgrove swore that Carteel and Goodside had resumed that argument later that afternoon, and that Carteel had sprung from his tent with knife in hand and stabbed Goodside in the breast.

The jury considered the evidence for only half an hour, then delivered the court a verdict of guilty.

Governor Edward Cornwallis, who presided at the trial, sentenced Peter Carteel to execution. On September 2, 1749, "in pursuance of the sentence of Death pronounced against him by the

General Court," Peter Carteel was led to a tree near the high-water mark and hanged.

Governor Cornwallis described the murder and execution in a report to the Lords of Trade in England. The Lords responded with the following: "Your method of proceeding in the trial of Peter Carteel for murder was very regular and proper, and will have a good effect, as it will convince the settlers of the intention of conforming to the laws and constitution of the mother country in every point."

The Lords of Trade were wrong. Criminals and murderers ran rampant in Halifax for many years to come. Hanging Peter Carteel, and many others in subsequent years, did not stop Halifax settlers from drinking their brains senseless and then robbing, stealing, brawling in the streets, and killing one another.

DOUGLAS THE BAD

The ship *Zero* was under full sail when Nova Scotia fishermen boarded her. They found no crew, the beams hacked and sawed, and the bottom bored with auger holes.

A few weeks later, in September 1865, there was drunken talk along the Halifax waterfront that linked the *Zero* with the word *piracy*. Fingers pointed at the first mate, an ugly, chicken-breasted man named Douglas. Gossip soon chased rumour like a dog in heat. The authorities heard what was being said and, with no further ado, hauled Douglas into jail, along with the ship's cook, a black man named Henry Doucey.

Doucey broke under questioning. He told the authorities that from the moment they weighed anchor, Douglas had it in for Captain Benson. Douglas had included Doucey in his plot to take the ship. Together, they entered the captain's quarters when he was asleep and hit him with a belaying pin, then they carried him on deck, sewed him into a piece of canvas, and threw him overboard.

As luck would have it, neither man was a competent sailor. After failing to sail the ship, they tried to scuttle her.

Doucey's confession got them convicted. They were both sentenced to hang, but at the last minute, Douglas received a conditional pardon. Some say the pardon was because Douglas was Protestant and Doucey was a Catholic, but more than likely it was because Douglas was white and Doucey was black.

Henry Doucey was hanged on January 24, 1866. He has the unenviable distinction of being the last man hanged for piracy in Canada.

Eleven years later, Douglas died in the penitentiary on Halifax's Northwest Arm. His body was turned over to the town surgeons for dissection. And until 1896, his vital organs were reserved at the Halifax Medical College, catalogued under the name "Douglas the Bad."

TWO LEFT FEET

Edward Brown was a loafer who wore coarse woollen breeches and dreamed of soft prunella. He preferred comfort to hard work, and a beggar's allowance to a steady job. He was also a man given to impulse, one who seldom considered the consequences of blind reflex.

In August 1803, Brown entered Frederick Major's shop in Halifax to buy a length of leather. Major went into his storeroom to fetch the calfskin.

That's when impulse elbowed reason aside and, with both his eyes tighter than a banker's purse, Edward Brown blindly submitted to reflex.

When the Frederick Major returned, he saw a bulge under Brown's cloak. Major took a fit, charged Brown with stealing, and shouted "Thief!" at the top of his lungs, attracting the attention of all within earshot—including a constable.

Brown denied being a thief. He claimed he had two English boots under his cloak, boots he had just bought from Smith's Tannery around the corner. A bystander ran to the tannery, made inquiries, and returned to Major's shop to announce that Mr. Smith denied selling anyone leather boots from his tannery that morning. Then the constable examined the boots. Both were for the left foot, and were different sizes. Sure enough, they matched two right-footed boots on the shelf behind the counter.

Brown tried to explain that a sudden, uncontrollable urge had grabbed hold of him and made him reach for the English boots. No one listened. Nor did the judge, who found him guilty of stealing two leather boots valued at eight shillings.

On September 12, 1803, Edward Brown bared his back at the whipping post in the market square and received thirty-nine lashes for petty theft. He then sat in the stocks for one hour, and had his left thumb branded with the letter *T*.

While he was in the stocks, passersby threw horse dung at him, and mocked him for being such a stupid, impulsive oaf that had no better sense than to think he had two left feet.

A WELL-TOLD LIE

In October 1776, outside the piazza—a covered wooden walkway at Halifax's Market Wharf—John O'Farrell pulled out his pocket watch to check the hour. William Brattle's eyes narrowed, and then his hand shot out and grabbed O'Farrell by the collar. Brattle insisted the watch was his, and that he had witnesses to prove it.

O'Farrell claimed he had paid a black woman for the watch, a servant by the name of Shaw who lived in the lower part of town. How she came by it, he did not know.

William Brattle meant to find out. With a magistrate in tow, he slogged through the muddy Halifax streets, asking about the servant woman named Shaw. He finally found her beating clothes on a rock beside the Freshwater Brook, a stream that ran through the upper part of Halifax.

Mrs. Shaw was a husky woman, hunched from hard work. She was wearing layers of hand-me-down clothes and had the empty facial expression of subservience. When the magistrate asked how she had come by the watch, Shaw replied that she had hoed it up in the back garden. The magistrate challenged: "How did you know just where to dig in order to find it?"

Mrs. Shaw shrugged compliantly, and told the magistrate that she knew where it was because she had watched her husband bury it.

Brattle and the magistrate now turned their attention on Peter Shaw.

Peter was stacking firewood near the south barracks when the magistrate challenged him to explain how he had come by William Brattle's watch. Peter removed his hat and smiled deferentially. He said he had found it—in his own coat pocket. Then Peter Shaw explained, in a voice that sounded too much like truth, that a few days ago, he had been lugging firewood to the officers' quarters inside the fort at the top of the hill. A soldier had stopped him when he entered through the main gate, and the two had jabbered for a bit. It was not until later that afternoon, after he had returned to his room, that he found the watch. The best he could figure, Peter said, was the soldier must have dropped that watch into his pocket.

As to burying the watch, Peter Shaw explained that he meant to return the watch to the soldier, but in the meantime, he did not want someone sneaking into his room and stealing it.

There was nothing cold and barren about Peter Shaw's version of events. He charged his words with emotion and filled them with meaning. The difficulty the trial judge had was in believing them. Sometimes truth is stranger than fiction—but most of the time, what seems too strange to believe is nothing more than a well-told lie.

On October 8, 1776, Peter Shaw had his left hand branded with the letter *T*, and his back chequered with "thirty lashes, well laid on."

MOSES HAZEN

Moses Hazen is a name that conjures the image of a bearded prophet serving a wrathful God. But Moses Hazen was no prophet. He was twenty-six years old, and a first lieutenant in Colonel Robert Monckton's company. They were stationed at Fort Frederick, at the mouth of the St. John River in what is now Saint John. He was an angry young man, as wrathful as his wrathful God—a plug of bad temper, with a meanness that clenched his fingers and blazed his eyes at the sight of snow-covered hillsides stained with blood.

In 1755, Governor Charles Lawrence ordered the expulsion of all Acadians from Nova Scotia. Acadians were French inhabitants who had fallen under British rule after the Treaty of Utrecht in 1713. At the instigation of agents from France, some of these Acadian settlers persisted in acts of violence against British soldiers. Governor Lawrence decided to punish all Acadians for the actions of a few.

Many Acadians escaped expulsion from Nova Scotia, and in the year or two following, they settled along the St. John River. But in 1758, these St. John Valley lands were granted to men who had served the British Crown during the French and Indian War, and the Acadian squatters had to go.

The job of getting rid of them fell to Colonel Robert Monckton. In the fall of 1758, he led a contingent up the St. John River as far as Gagetown, destroying the new Acadian settlements and shooing their occupiers farther up the St. John River.

And this is where Moses Hazen comes in.

Early in 1759, he was commanding Fort Frederick, a little post in Saint John, and on February 18, he set off upriver to complete Monckton's work.

A lieutenant name Butler, who was stationed at Fort Frederick, left a letter dated March 6, 1759, that told of Hazen's exploits in or near St. Ann's (the site of present-day Fredericton).

Hazen's company of soldiers found two villages creased in silence and abandoned. The French inhabitants had fled to the woods, herding their livestock ahead of them. The soldiers followed the tracks for a kilometre or so, then returned to fire the Acadians' dwelling houses, churches, barns, stables, and granaries. When they left, the villages were heaps of charred timbers and toppled walls.

The following morning, the soldiers tramped through heavy snow toward a small settlement down river where the French inhabitants were all at home. The soldiers crept close to this cluster of homes— close enough to see a woman fill a bucket of water from a hole chopped in the river ice and lug it back to a square-log house. A man split firewood beside a barn. Two other men herded three cows away from the tree line at the far side of the settlement, and into a stable.

The soldiers crept closer. They could now smell chimney smoke, and hear a child's laugh and a woman's song. A wattle fence creaked against the drifting snow, and ice scoured the shore. On Hazen's whispered order, the soldiers primed and charged their muskets and fixed their bayonets.

Moses Hazen, his face twisted with malice, signalled his troops forward. A hundred stubbled soldiers—blanket-wrapped against the cold, with their boots muffled by rags—rose slowly, and waded across a snow-blown field splintered with cornstalks.

There was no drumbeat. No command to fire. Just a sudden explosion that startled the grey morning light, hushed the wind, and filled the air with the smell of cordite. The soldiers recharged their pieces while howling hell into the hearts of the Acadian settlers. Men, women, and children ran from their homes and through the blue smoke to escape from the ransack of their lives.

Near a snuggle of houses, three Acadian men stood their ground with sickles and scythes. They were helpless at the sudden attack, and hopeless with their workaday weapons that were better suited to cutting salt hay than hacking through flesh and bone. Another volley, and all three spun and fell, their arms and legs twisting with regret. Two were still alive when the soldiers took their scalps. The soldiers cinched the raw trophies to their black leather belts. Each scalp was a tangle of black hair and wet flesh.

Hazen and his murderous band pursued the Acadians into the woods, and caught four men, three women, and four children. Then they returned to the village and, at Hazen's command, torched the houses and outbuildings, and threw the cattle and the bodies of the murdered Acadians into the flames.

For the soldiers, their return trip to Fort Frederick was silent. Their feet slowed to a troubled pace as though half awake. Hesitant through the gate, awkward at the male and female scalps dangling from their belts. How hurried these soldiers had been to march from this fort, keen for killing. How pallid they returned. Uncertain. Wavering. Like leash men sniffing the stink that traced their boot prints in the new fallen snow.

OLD MAN'S DREAM

In 1849, Daniel Kerr of Dalhousie, New Brunswick, received a letter from someone who remained anonymous. The writer claimed he'd had a disturbing dream in which he saw John Kerr, Daniel's brother, being murdered along a riverbank. John Kerr had been gone for almost a year. He had joined a logging gang in Miramichi, and never returned home.

The letter told Daniel Kerr that the dream was so vivid it must be true. The writer told of seeing John Kerr leaving a barn with another man. There was a white house nearby, and a footpath that led down to the river, where the unknown man used a handspike (a crowbar) to bludgeon John Kerr. The unknown man then drew a knife and stabbed Kerr to death.

That was enough to stir Daniel into making inquiries at the logging camp. He discovered that his brother had left the camp with a Pictou County man named McFayden. Daniel wrote a letter to the sheriff of Pictou County, in which he detailed the mysterious letter writer's dream. The sheriff wrote back that a partially decomposed body had been found near Moose River with a handspike alongside it. Its identity was unknown.

Daniel's letter now had the sheriff wondering about the dreamer. Was he simply a man who'd had a richly vivid dream? Or had he actually been an eyewitness to the murder and did not want his name involved in the case? The sheriff started his own investigation, and learned that a local man named Neil McFayden had been wearing a jacket with the name *John Kerr* stitched on the outside of the collar. When the sheriff went to McFayden's farm, he saw that the house, the barn, and the footpath to the river matched the dreamer's description to a T. Inside McFayden's house, he found a pair of shoes with Kerr's name on the inside.

The sheriff confronted McFayden with details of the murder as they were written in the letter—details that only someone who had been on the riverbank at the time of the murder could possibly know. McFayden crumbled, figuring someone had witnessed the event. He said that he and John Kerr had argued, and that Kerr had attacked him first. He claimed he had used the handspike in self-defence against a man twice his size.

The sheriff now had McFayden for manslaughter. But a jury would never convict him, given that John Kerr had been a mountain of a man. If Kerr had started the fight, Neil McFayden had every right to defend himself with a handspike.

Then the sheriff remembered another detail in Daniel Kerr's letter: the dreamer had recorded dreaming of a man bludgeoning John Kerr from behind and *then* stabbing him to death. The letter even described the knife as having a long blade and a rough buckskin handle.

John Kerr's head had been so badly smashed that the sheriff had simply assumed bludgeoning was the cause of death—especially since the handspike was found lying alongside Kerr's body. The sheriff had not noticed a knife wound when he first found Kerr. But the coroner, John McKay, did see it. It was a clean slit in Kerr's back.

The sheriff returned to the McFayden farm, and this time he spoke to McFayden's wife. Yes, indeed, she said, her husband had a long-bladed knife. It was something like a dirk, with a buckskin handle.

When the sheriff returned to the jail, he withdrew the knife from a pouch and showed it to McFayden. Now believing the sheriff knew much more than he did—and that he had an eyewitness, not just circumstantial evidence—McFayden broke down and confessed to murdering John Kerr in cold blood.

The letter writer never came forward, so we are left to decide for ourselves whether he dreamed the details of a murder that had actually taken place, or if he was at McFayden's farm, followed McFayden and Kerr down to the riverbank, and witnessed the murder. But there's something else: Daniel Kerr only assumed the letter writer was a man. It could just as easily have been a woman—perhaps even Neil McFayden's wife.

WELDON THE RAGMAN

In October 1752, Dick Weldon kicked through Halifax's dry streets. His dusty breeches were unbuttoned at the knee, and his grimy grey stockings were rolled to the ankle. Weldon was a grumble of discontent because a smuggler's boat was anchored in the harbour, bound for Boston on the next tide, and he had nothing to sell.

He kicked at a hardened clump of horse dung in the dust, and cursed out loud at Jack Frazier for getting hanged the week before. Frazier's hanging had scared the hell out of Halifax's thieves and burglars, and had them sitting quietly on their hands. For a ragman—a buyer and seller of stolen goods—like Weldon, it was damn near impossible to find something stolen or smuggled to buy. Weldon cursed Jack Frazier again, and kicked at another clump.

Weldon went to bed cursing, and woke up cursing an hour later. This time, he was cursing at whomever was calling his name and knocking at his door. He blindly negotiated his way across the one-room house to the window, passing a chair, a deal table, and the fireplace full of sleeping coals. He pulled aside a ratty curtain that hung over the glass. Outside on the street, a redcoat soldier anxiously looked from corner to corner before cupping his hands at his mouth and calling again for Weldon to open the door. He identified himself as Tom Jobbett, and said two others had come along with him.

Except for the soldier's grey-white breeches and conical cap, Weldon could see little else but shadow. He reached for a powder horn and a pistol from a hanger beside the door, and rammed home the powder and shot. Then he swung the door open and, with his pistol, gestured for the three to enter.

Without turning his back to the thieves, Weldon fetched a coal from the fireplace, blew on it, and lit a candle. The men all had dirty, unshaven faces and wore ragged clothes—including Jobbett, whose uniform gave him the look of a soldier who was a long time absent from duty. Each man had wrapped scraps of filthy cloth around his hands for warmth.

Jobbett was their spokesman. He said they had barrels of flour and pork to sell. They rolled them forward and Weldon lowered the candle to have a look. The light revealed the king's broad arrow stamped on the barrel staves. The flour was moist from the damp night air, and the pork had greenish mould at the edges.

Nevertheless, this was just the sort of goods Weldon preferred: unidentifiable, except for the barrel staves, which would later make a fine fire on the hearth.

Weldon and Jobbett negotiated a deal at thirty shillings, and not a penny more.

By dawn, a storm blew heavy from the harbour mouth. It swamped dinghies and yawls, whipped sheets of water over the wharves and warehouses, and transformed the streets into criss-crossing rivers of treacle.

Masters and seamen went scrambling over boats that pitched wildly at the docks. They changed handholds on the rope lines, fighting against a grey-green sea that pounded and swooped at their ship's gunnels. They fixed gratings on hatchways, and nailed tar-paulins over them to keep the seawater away from the stowed cargo below. Their brisk hands greased marlinspikes around, over, and through tarred ropes, knotting bights in the ropes to belay the deck gear and canvas. When all was battened and stayed, another blow would barrel down the harbour, billow seawater over the bow and forecastle, and undo what the seamen had long been labouring to do.

Dick Weldon trudged along the waterfront, hunched forward against the wind with his coattails flapping like a gull's wings. He was disappointed at not finding a buyer for the pork and flour. The captains knew it would take two days before the storm blew out and the sea settled, and they wanted no part in stowing stolen goods any longer than it took to clear the beacon at Sandwich Point.

Weldon entered his shack with his clothes and spirit both sop-ping. Rain dripped from the chimney funnel and hissed on the low-burning coals on the grate. Downdrafts skirled the smoke about the room where it rose and hung on the ceiling boards.

Weldon had one last option for getting rid of the stolen goods: William Van Telson, a general merchant, and a penny pincher who could bargain the devil into lowering the heat in hell.

Van Telson hemmed and hawed before buying a small amount of what Weldon had to sell. Weldon wanted twenty shillings for half the flour and pork. Van Telson paid three halfpennies for two pounds of the flour because it was wet, and three halfpence per pound for ninety pounds of pork.

Weldon had taken a loss—but that wasn't the worst of it. When he returned to his shack, Ann Pentenny was waiting for him in the alley. Pentenny, an indentured servant to Mrs. Birch, had a silk handkerchief to sell. She had news as well. She said a thief had robbed the king's stores the night before, and had left behind the bayonet he used to pry open the shutters. Bill Foy, the provost marshal, was now searching the taverns for Tom Jobbett.

Weldon's jaw slackened. He pulled at his face, looked at the remaining two bow-bellied barrels in the corner of the room, and mumbled something about being a gravedigger who was up to his ass in bad business. Without wasting another moment, he hurried Ann Pentenny out the door, fetched two gunny sacks from a wooden chest, and filled them with flour. He lugged the sacks—one over each shoulder—to the downgrade to the waterfront and dumped the flour into the gutter. He paused long enough to watch the white water run down the hill to the harbour. Then he went back for another load, and carried two more bags to the gutter. The rain-soaked sacks stretched under the weight of the pasty flour. It dribbled in chalky splotches in the mud behind Weldon.

The pork was next. Weldon spent more than an hour hauling sacks of pork to a newly dug ditch near the palisade.

Now he only had the barrel staves to burn. Back home, Weldon stirred the grate to get a fire going. Caked-on ash clung to the irons, and his poker raised only a faint, mouldy-smelling smoke. The dripping chimney had dowsed the coals beyond rekindling.

Weldon went the colour of winter birch. His hands trembled as he fumbled with flint and steel. Spark after spark danced about his hands, whirling themselves extinct before they ever reached the dried kindling. He struck the stone harder, faster. The sparks doubled, and one suddenly leaped among the tinder. It flared for an instant, then smouldered. Weldon nuzzled close to the grate and whispered his breath over the smother.

Just then, a rap at the door jerked his head and hands from the struggling fire. A voice boomed from the street, ordering Dick Weldon to open in the name of King George. The ragman ran to the window. In the grey twilight, he saw Bill Foy, the provost Marshal, standing outside with six soggy redcoats. Beyond them, under the eaves of a neighbouring house, Weldon saw the lean face of William Van Telson.

Within a week, Weldon was tried by the Supreme Court and convicted of stealing from the king's stores. He was sentenced to hang on Friday, November 20, 1752. Jobbett, Dean, and Belcher received the same sentence.

When the time for the hangings finally came, at one o'clock on the afternoon of November 20, Dick Weldon drew up his body with what little courage he had left, and fell into line behind the three thieves for the march from the jailhouse to the gallows. According to the *Halifax Gazette*, Weldon's step was unsteady going up the stairs, and his voice was weak when he told the spectators that he died "in Charity with all men."

Tom Jobbett begged forgiveness for his crime, and warned his fellow soldiers to avoid sin and drink. Belcher and Dean held their silence.

When the hangman set the noose, Weldon's legs wobbled and his body shook uncontrollably. The hangman grabbed the rope for a strong pull. Weldon's tongue sprang from his mouth. His neck stretched, his legs kicked, and a cough stuck in his throat.

PATRICIDE

Donald Campbell's mother had only been dead a year when his father, Hugh Campbell, returned from Halifax with a new wife. The woman's name was Christian, and she was good-looking and ten years younger than her new husband.

The Campbells lived in Rogers Hill in Pictou County, Nova Scotia. Hugh Campbell owned a sizable farm, and Donald's farm was three kilometres from his father's.

Donald was a tall, strapping lad, and a hard worker who meant to make something important of himself and the Campbell name. He sometimes bragged that one day, when his father died, the whole of Rogers Hill would belong to him.

But now Hugh Campbell had another wife, and Donald feared the Campbell family farm would go to her when his father died. Donald brooded day and night over the thought of being disinherited. Soon the possibility turned into a probability, and then into a sure thing. He agonized as he watched his stepmother fuss about his father during Sunday meals, and winced when his father nuzzled her cheek in a way he had never done with Donald's mother.

On the night of March 17, 1819, Donald could not bear the torment any longer. He went to his father's house intending to shoot his father and stepmother both. But his mind was so lathered that his hands fumbled with the musket, and when the flint fell out, he couldn't find it. So he set the house on fire instead, then grabbed a club from the woodpile and waited by the door for his father and stepmother to run from the flames.

He clubbed his stepmother a vicious blow that opened her skull. Then he struck his father. The first blow caught the old man across the shoulders and drove him down onto one knee. Hugh Campbell reached out and grabbed his son's coat. Donald pushed him away and swung from his heels. His old father collapsed in a pool of blood.

Donald dropped the club and dragged the bodies into the flames. At the sound of neighbours coming to help fight the fire, Donald ran home and did not return.

For months, Hugh Campbell's new young wife had been the talk of the county—including how their marriage might cut Donald out of all he thought he deserved. That's why his not showing up when his father's house was on fire raised suspicion among the neighbours.

For many of them, the blood-smeared club they found on Hugh's property only confirmed what they suspected: murder.

The sheriff discovered more incriminating evidence. A button found at the murder scene matched one missing from Donald's coat, and the flint dropped in the dooryard neatly fit Donald's musket. And when Donald answered the sheriff's knock, the first thing he noticed was that Donald's hands were badly burned.

The jury did not take long to convict Donald Campbell. And on the gallows, he confessed all.

The Romans had a unique punishment for a man who murdered his father. They beat him severely, then, while he was still alive, sewed him into a large leather bag with a poisonous snake, and threw him into a river.

Donald Campbell had a noose put around his neck, dropped from the gallows, and died within minutes. By Roman standards, he got off easy.

UNRULY DARTMOUTH

Long-time Halifax residents often joke about needing a passport to cross the harbour bridges to the Dartmouth side. There are still some Haligonians who go to Dartmouth unwillingly, and only if it is absolutely necessary. Then there are the very few who won't go at all. Some of these people consider Dartmouth a traffic maze, a virtual rabbit warren that is impossible to navigate. Others think of it as unruly.

In 1751, John William Hoffman, a Justice of the Peace, thought the Dartmouth side of the harbour was the most unruly place on earth. He had good reason.

Camped in Dartmouth was a gang of thugs called Gorham's Rangers, an army unit comprised of New England riff-raff and hooligans. The Rangers had an unsavoury reputation for hard drinking and extreme violence. These were the soldiers Governor Edward Cornwallis had commissioned to hunt and scalp the Mi'kmaq.

On October 12, 1751, John Hoffman rowed from Halifax to Dartmouth with four arrest warrants tucked inside his shirt. The newly arrived German settlers had complained that Walter Clark, a Dartmouth tavern owner, had forced them to install shingles on his house on Sunday, in violation of the Sabbath law. Hoffman also had a warrant against Walter Clark for selling liquor on Sundays.

Serving these warrants would be troublesome enough. Walter Clark and his wife Mary were mangy, hard-mouthed individuals who could flay one's flesh with the sheer coarseness of their language. Walter had a face perpetually punched forward in defiance, and Mary was a fiery harpy with a voice that could cut wood.

But it was the two other warrants that pestered John Hoffman the most. One was against Corporal Francis Hamilton, for an assault he had committed in a Halifax tavern. Hamilton served in Captain Proctor's company as a member of Gorham's Rangers.

The other warrant was against Captain Clapham, for forcing German settlers to cut wood on Sundays. Clapham was also a member of Gorham's Rangers, and well respected among the Rangers for his brutish behaviour.

Hoffman caught the verbal abuse he had expected from Walter and Mary. Then he walked into the Ranger camp and confronted Corporal Hamilton. Hamilton was a no-account soldier, and not much better than the company he kept. He refused to accept Hoffman's charge, and threatened to take a fireplace poker to Hoffman's head.

That's when Ensign Francis Gilbert entered the fray. He defended Hamilton's right to fight with anyone he had a mind to. Then he praised Captain Clapham for forcing those damn beggarly Germans to work, Sunday or not. Gilbert cursed John Hoffman a blue streak then ordered five soldiers to arrest him and bind him with ropes. The Rangers marched Hoffman through the Dartmouth streets like a common criminal, pushing him, whipping him, and mocking him before all who crowded to watch. Many civilians got into the act by adding their hands to the pushing and slapping.

At last the mob stopped at Clark's Tavern, where Walter and Mary joined their voices to the abuse and their hands to the beating of John Hoffman. Mary tore at Hoffman's clothes, stripping him of his coat and lowering his breeches. All the while she shouted: "Where is your honour now?"

Gilbert and the Ranger Company tortured John Hoffman for nearly two hours then threw him into a rowboat and sent him back across the harbour, where they said he belonged.

The gang of Rangers eventually faced the charges John Hoffman had brought with him to Dartmouth, as well as the additional ones of unlawful confinement and striking against the "will of government."

However, in 1751, soldiers, no matter how unruly, were a valuable asset to the Halifax settlement, especially against the threat of attack from the French and their Mi'kmaw allies. When Governor Hobbs heard of the charges against the soldiers in Gorham's Rangers, and the circumstances surrounding them, he dismissed the charges at once and ordered Ensign Gilbert simply to apologize to John Hoffman. The rule of law had been shunted aside for the expediency of keeping soldiers at their posts. And John Hoffman failed to receive any redress for the abuse he suffered in Dartmouth.

CARING KINFOLK

(BJG)

Margarita Ariana Jekyll Saunders was born in England in 1790, moving to New Brunswick shortly after her birth. She was the eldest child (and easily the cleverest) born to John Saunders, the man who would serve as New Brunswick's chief justice from 1822 until his death in 1834.

She lived most of her life on Fredericton's Shore Street, a short street in the oldest part of the town. It is so called not because it leads to the banks of the St. John River, but because at one time, most of it was owned by George Shore, a member of the 104th Regiment who distinguished himself in the War of 1812—and who was Margarita's husband.

By 1867, Margarita, now a long-time widow, was getting on in years. One of her closest friends was Horatia Ewing, an English novelist and the wife of Major Rex Ewing, who was stationed in Fredericton.

In the winter of that year, Margarita fell ill. It was probably of nothing more than a bad cold. Two of Margarita's relatives— her nephew John Saunders and the woman Mrs. Ewing called "his wooden wife"—made themselves their aunt's keepers. They knew Margarita Shore had some money and a considerable amount of property.

The Saunders pair stationed themselves in the parlour at the foot of the stairs that lead to Margarita's room, and as each of the old lady's many friends called, they got the same story:

"Oh, we're sorry, but it's no use. The poor thing is so weak. She'd probably not know you. She's nearly gone, you know. We've really given up hope."

And so the sorrowing visitor departed.

Reverend John Medley was bishop of Fredericton at the time. He suspected something was amiss, and when he went to visit Margarita, he got the same treatment as her other friends. But Medley was an Englishman, and one made of very stern stuff. He thundered at the Saunders pair, "Mrs. Shore is of my flock. I am her shepherd. And I will see her!" With that, he brushed aside Joseph and his wife, and up the stairs he went.

Moments later, he called for a pitcher of water and a tumbler. From within his episcopal robes, he withdrew a bottle of brandy.

It worked wonders. In jig time, Margarita Shore was downstairs fixing herself something to eat—for her deeply concerned relatives had been slowly starving her to death.

As Mrs. Ewing told it, Joseph Saunders and his "wooden wife" were asked to leave, which they did promptly. And Margarita Ariana Jekyll Saunders Shore was left to spend a good while longer on earth, in peace and contentment and without further "help" from her caring kin.

THE MURDER OF EDWARD HOW

In 1750, the British and French were not at war, but neither were they on the best of terms. Even the common soldier knew it was just a matter of time before each side would be eyeing the other along the barrel of a musket.

This tension surrounded the negotiations that Edward How conducted with the French in Beausejour. He was trying to secure the release of several English prisoners held by the French. The negotiations were going slowly, with the French bargaining for the exchange of more French prisoners than the number of English ones they were willing to release.

Edward How probably understood better than most how each side tried to gain the upper hand by getting more than they gave. In 1746, Edward How himself had been wounded and captured during the Battle of Grand Pré, and was later exchanged for six French prisoners. He knew that officers always traded at a premium, and high-ranking bureaucrats fetched significantly more than two men for one.

So during these negotiations on the banks of the Missaguash River, How drove a hard bargain. On October 4, 1750, he was returning to British lines after one of these parleys, still under a flag of truce, when a shot rang out. How staggered into the tall marsh grass and fell dead. He had been shot in the back.

The English refused to believe the French had engaged in such treachery—so they blamed an Acadian man named Étienne Batard and a Mi'kmaq man named Jean Baptiste Cope. Both denied the accusation. And to this day, no one knows for certain who murdered Edward How.

However, at the time, suspicion was enough to fire British hearts with a passionate distrust of the Acadians and the Mi'kmaq—a distrust that marked their relations for years to come, and would later play a part in the expulsion of more than ten thousand Acadians from Nova Scotia.

MASS MURDER

(BJG)

A drawknife is a sharp, heavy blade about two feet long with a handle fitted downward from each end. Carpenters often used it to round off the corners of squared lumber; others used it to peel pulpwood. And midway through the nineteenth century, one was used to commit the bloodiest mass murder in New Brunswick history.

About all that's known of William Kerrigan is that he was an Irish immigrant born in 1804, that he settled near Westfield (a few kilometres upriver from Saint John), that he had a family, and that he went suddenly and violently insane.

Around one o'clock in the morning on Sunday, December 12, 1851, Kerrigan roused his twelve-year-old son to fetch Mrs. William McClusky, Mr. and Mrs. William Waggoner, and John C. McLaughlin, and ask them to come over. He said he was sick. Everyone came.

When they arrived, Kerrigan greeted them warmly, and asked McLaughlin to sing a hymn as they all knelt in prayer. Then Kerrigan took a drawknife from a cupboard and gashed McLaughlin along the side of the head. The wounded man fled. Kerrigan gave him chase to the front door, then returned to the house and butchered everyone else he had summoned, as well as his own wife and family.

McLaughlin roused the neighbours. The first to arrive was Alexander Long—a big fellow who came armed with a double-bitter. That's an axe.

Kerrigan saw the axe and escaped towards the river in the dark. His neighbours found him about ten hours later, crouched near a fence beside the St. John River. He was wearing only a cotton shirt and trousers—and he was frozen solid. Through one hour's madness, William Kerrigan left two households filled with sadness, and his own filled with silence.

FORGERY

Miles O'Brien was a Halifax labourer who could not hold a steady job. He was lazy, and he liked to drink.

In June 1796, Miles found several bills of exchange blowing across a muddy Halifax street. Bills of exchange were promissory notes. The person named on the note received a particular sum of money when that person presented the bill to the appropriate lending house or merchant. It was an early form of the common cheque.

Robert Bolland's name was on the bills, and he had received them from Nathaniel Phillip of St. John's, Newfoundland. Phillip had issued them to Bolland as payment for trade goods. The merchants authorized to make payment were William Lyons and Thomas Boggs of Halifax.

After finding the bills of exchange, and hiding them under the floorboards of his shack in the upper part of town, Miles O'Brien ruminated about them for days. He slowly convinced himself that his luck had changed for the better. All he had to do was present them to Lyons and Boggs, forge Bolland's name on the reverse sides, and walk away with a pocket full of hard cash.

Most criminals are dumb. And they are impulsive. They usually don't take the time to think through all the details of their intended crime.

What O'Brien had not counted on was that Robert Bolland was well known at the office of Lyons and Boggs, and that his signature was easily recognized there. When O'Brien presented the bills of exchange with Bolland's name forged on them, the clerk serving him called for a magistrate immediately.

Miles O'Brien went to trial on October 18, 1796. He offered no defence, and within minutes, the judge declared him guilty. O'Brien was sentenced to one year in jail. He would also have to stand one hour in the pillory, and have one ear cut off.

Slicing off an ear was a common punishment for forgery and counterfeiting. The practice dates back to medieval times, when counterfeiting involved altering the ownership brand on a livestock animal's ear. Cutting off a forger or counterfeiter's ear and nailing it to the pillory was an effective means of reminding a criminal about the details of his crime. And to the benefit of the general public, it marked the culprit as a person who could not be trusted.

There were other cases of forgers and counterfeiters losing an ear to Nova Scotia authorities. In March 1817, in Halifax, Mary Foley had one of her ears removed for counterfeiting silver dollars in a wooden mould. And in December 1835, Moses Lacey was caught passing counterfeit coin. He served one year in the county jail, stood one hour in the pillory, and had one ear sliced off and the wound cauterized with a hot iron.

By the mid-nineteenth century, such corporal punishment was on the way out in Nova Scotia. In 1851, the revised statutes for the province now stated: "Judgement or sentence shall not be given and awarded against any person convicted of any offence, that such person do suffer the punishment of being set in the pillory or of having his ears nailed thereto or cut off, or do suffer punishment of being whipped."

PORK BARREL MURDER

There is no armour against fate, and, as Daniel Defoe wrote, man cannot suspend it.

John Dunbar was a disbanded Loyalist soldier who lived with his wife near Mill Cove, outside St. Stephen, New Brunswick. A nearby hill still bears his name. He and his wife had a rocky relationship. The rumour was that he had married her only for her money—which wasn't much, but enough that he would tolerate marital misery in the hope of getting his hands on whatever there was.

In 1785, neighbours missed seeing Mrs. Dunbar around her cabin, and wondered at not hearing the couple's high-pitched bickering day and night. Dunbar said his wife had gone to Nova Scotia to visit relatives.

After a couple months, when Mrs. Dunbar had not returned, the neighbours became suspicious. They notified Sheriff John Dunn, who questioned Dunbar and then searched the premises. He found nothing in Dunbar's cabin. But as fate would have it, just as Sheriff Dunn was about to leave, he saw a small door leading down to a cold cellar. The sheriff descended the ladder. First he saw the usual stores of root vegetables in sand-filled wooden boxes. Then he pointed to a large barrel in a dark corner.

Dunbar went white, and said it contained salt pork.

But Sheriff Dunn heard the catch in Dunbar's voice. He wasn't buying it. He pried up the cover and took a look himself.

Mixed in with the pork roasts and chops were the dismembered remains of Mrs. Dunbar, pickled in a strong brine made from the best Turks Island salt.

John Dunbar confessed on the spot, and again at his trial. He had killed his wife in a drunken rage, he said, for a stash of gold coins she kept hidden in the cellar.

Now, it seems the authorities had difficulty keeping John Dunbar confined. He escaped twice before his execution. Each time he widened the soft iron bars of his jail cell and slipped free. The second time, he crossed the St. Stephen–Calais border into the United States, where all trace of him was lost.

Some years later, however, fate, unable to be suspended, caught up with John Dunbar. A Mr. Bentley of St. Stephen was visiting Boston. He went out walking and was struck on the head by a falling shingle. When he looked up, he was amazed to recognize John Dunbar busily repairing a roof. Mr. Bentley informed the Boston authorities, and in due course, John Dunbar was returned to New Brunswick, where he was hanged for murdering his wife and stuffing her dismembered corpse into a barrel of salt pork.

CALL IT MURDER!

Peregrine White hated his neighbour James Rogers so much that he died for it.

Both men were elderly, foul-mouthed, and vindictive. They had spent most of their long lives in rural Kings County, New Brunswick, in spiting at and vilifying one another.

Things came to a head one day in September 1810 when James Rogers's dog barked at Peregrine White. That brought on a verbal slanging match. The name-calling got so hot that it roused most of their neighbours, including Rogers's son-in-law, a man named Bill Masculine.

Masculine strode out of his house with a musket on his shoulder. Rogers pointed at Peregrine White and ordered his son-in-law to shoot him. Masculine did, putting a musket ball in White's thigh. White died a week later, and the law charged Masculine with murder.

At his trial, Masculine claimed he did not aim to kill, but shot for the leg. James Rogers took the stand in Masculine's defence, and said Peregrine White had asked for it anyway. It seems the jury sympathized with Masculine, and was willing to change the charge from murder to manslaughter.

But Judge Ward Chipman would have nothing to do with a reduced charge. He overruled the jury, and ordered them to "call it murder" and deliver a guilty verdict.

The jury did its duty, after which Judge Chipman did his. He sentenced Bill Masculine to hang. And all because James Rogers's dog had barked at Peregrine White.

GOBLIN'S HOLLOW

It was a clear spring night on May 12, 1859, when Ann Beaton, a forty-one-year-old spinster from Lyndale, Prince Edward Island, walked down the Murray Harbour Road and never returned. The community searched for two days, but it was not until eleven o'clock in the morning on the second day that her brother, Murdock, found her body less than five hundred feet from her home, in an overgrown gulley known as Goblin's Hollow. Beside her was a blood-smeared grubbing hoe. The coroner found sixteen wounds to her head, neck, and mouth.

The local newspaper reported: "Her brains were knocked out, and her teeth driven in, and her mouth horribly cut."

A criminal investigation proved fruitless. There were no eyewitnesses. There was no motive. There was nothing but a garden hoe, and most households had several of those. The coroner's inquest ruled: "Wilful Murder by some person or persons at present Unknown."

For the first time in their lives, people in that settlement bolted their doors at night. There is nothing more frightening than believing that one of your own is a murderer. The people demanded a second inquiry. This one lasted two days, and revealed that the blood-smeared grubbing hoe belonged to Angus Matheson.

Matheson, along with his wife and son, were committed to jail in Charlottetown, but later released because of insufficient evidence.

After the failed police investigation, the people decided to apply their own means for discovering the truth. According to highland superstition, a victim's wounds will bleed whenever the murderer places his or her hand on the body. Every adult in the district attended Ann Beaton's wake, and one by one they touched her body— but no blood appeared.

There were those who said Ann Beaton was a mother without being a wife, and that a jealous woman followed her down the Murray Harbour Road, lured her into Goblin's Hollow, and took her life. But that could not be proved.

Ann Beaton's murder has forever remained a mystery. For years after, a night alone in Goblin's Hollow became a means for testing the courage of Lyndale's boys.

The girls had their own ritual. They would walk down the Murray Harbour Road singing this song:

The lassies that lived there in Lyndale,
Will milk before twilight will dwindle.
And they'll cast wary eyes at the cross where she lies,
Where sounds are heard there unearthly, they say.
Where sounds are heard there unearthly.

THE TRIAL OF CAPTAIN RICHARD CROSS

A jury must determine innocence or guilt by sifting fact from fancy. In the case against Captain Richard Cross, fancy comprised the better part of the evidence.

On the morning of December 26, 1825, in Halifax, two soldiers who were returning to the barracks after celebrating Christmas Day found Edward Shey, a former schoolmaster, dead in the snow outside the officers' quarters at the north barracks. An eyewitness fingered Captain Richard Cross as having murdered Shey.

Mr. Archibald prosecuted the case. The evidence against Captain Cross rested on the credibility of the eyewitness, Margaret Hall, a whore who knew her way around the barracks as well as any light bob. Margaret Hall was also a black woman. She testified to having gone to the officers' quarters that night on business with Mr. McDowell. While waiting outside his door, she heard a voice shout: "Walk off!" She recognized the voice of Captain Cross, and, thinking he was turning a woman out, descended the stairs to take a peek. She saw Captain Cross holding a candle with one hand, and dragging an old man wearing blue trousers and a round hat with the other. Without letting the old man go, Cross set the candle on a ledge. Then he carried the old man from the barracks and dropped him into a snowdrift beside the well.

Margaret Hall said that McDowell returned shortly after, and she remained with him in his room for nearly an hour and a half. When she left the barracks, the old man was still lying by the well.

William Sawyer represented Captain Cross. He dismissed Margaret Hall's testimony on the grounds that she bore a grudge against the captain. Sawyer established that three weeks earlier, Captain Cross had thrown Margaret Hall out of the barracks for "attempting to clap every man jack in the regiment." In other words, he thought she would give the soldiers gonorrhea. He had threatened to "scald her black arse" should she return.

The defence then called two of the captain's fellow officers to take the stand—two comrades in the same fraternity. It has been said that the devil would be blind a year and a day before one officer testified against another, yet the prosecution failed to object to the officers' favourable testimony on the captain's behalf.

Ensigns Costello and O'Brien both alleged that between one and two o'clock on the morning of December 26, they had discarded an old man from the downstairs hallway of the officers' quarters. The old man had been drunk, and singing loudly. After first summoning Captain Cross from his room, the three officers carried the old man to the front porch, and bolted the door against his return. How he had died, they knew not.

The jury retired for a short time, and returned with a verdict of not guilty.

The verdict seems reasonable enough, since the prosecution's eyewitness held a prejudice against the captain, and the defence's star witnesses were biased in his favour. In other words, both the testimonies for and against Captain Cross were heavily weighted with fancy.

The trial judge's closing remarks were every bit as fanciful. When discharging the prisoner, Judge Brynton Haliburton said: "Your reputation is not ruined; not only was the evidence not sufficient, but Margaret Hall's testimony was not credible. You return to an honourable profession, an unspotted man and free from suspicion."

How "unspotted" a whoring officer's reputation remains is a matter for moral conjecture. But stating that Captain Cross was free from suspicion based on the favourable testimony of two friends and fellow officers suggests the judge held his own prejudice: that a black woman's eyewitness testimony was no match for that of the two white military officers.

JOHN CRUTCH

John Crutch was well into his seventies, a corny-faced old codger who had the look of Lazarus come back from the grave. In November 1824, he stood before a Halifax court charged with raping and having carnal knowledge of a young girl named Elizabeth Burke.

On the girl's evidence, the jury determined that Crutch had not penetrated her, but only spilled his seed upon her body. For this indecent violence, the judge sentenced him to stand one hour in the pillory and serve three years in the Bridewell, Halifax's house of correction.

Haligonians were outraged at the sentence, and the *Acadian Recorder* newspaper suggested that the law should demand its full pound of flesh. On November 9, after the pillory had been erected in the market square, and before the appearance of the convicted criminal, a man stepped forward and delivered a speech that inflamed the passions of the many spectators gathered in the square. The man called for nothing less than a rope and a low tree limb for Jack Crutch.

The sheriff intervened and, after threatening the mob with a charge of riotous behaviour, led John Crutch to the pillory. The sight of Crutch further antagonized the crowd.

Crutch must have anticipated rough justice from the spectators, because under his clothes, he had strapped two boards on his chest and back, and fitted stovepipes over his arms and legs. A black iron kettle protected his head.

Once in the pillory, with his arms and legs restrained, Crutch was fair game for whatever the angry mob wanted to throw at him.

For an hour, a barrage of rotten potatoes, eggs, animal dung, and even stones was hurled at the prisoner. Two black eyes and a variety of cuts marked the dead accuracy of the crowd's aim.

Afterwards, the sheriff marched Crutch into the house of correction, where hardened prisoners would have three years to exact their anger on this seedy old reprobate.

CONVICTS

Richard Todd sailed the ship *Bower* out of Liverpool, England, and landed in Halifax, Nova Scotia, in early December 1752. He was bound for South Carolina, but wanted to unload his cargo in Nova Scotia. Winter had settled in, and Todd wanted to do the same in Halifax.

Nova Scotia needed settlers, Todd explained to the authorities. He had been paid by England to transport settlers to the colonies, and Halifax was every bit as needy a place to unload his cargo as South Carolina.

Governor Peregrine Hobson, who had recently replaced Edward Cornwallis as governor of Nova Scotia, knew full well that the colony needed settlers—but not necessarily the kind Richard Todd had to offer. Todd's settlers were the off-scourings of English prisons.

Hobson wrote the Lords of Trade in England to explain his refusal of Richard Todd's cargo of convicts.

"This province being so differently circumstanced from those to which Convicts are generally carried, we having no backcountry or hard labour to send them to, and besides are as yet so much in our infancy, that we have enough to do to keep a due observance of the Law and promote descent and moral behaviour in those settlers we have already."

WHO KILLED MARTHA CLOUGH?

Shortly before the evening on January 23, 1790, Marguery Baird sent her twelve-year-old daughter from a previous marriage, Martha Clough, to fetch tea and sugar from Mrs. John Pyke and molasses from Mrs. Brow. Both houses were a little more than a ten-minute walk away. Martha crossed the snow-covered field behind Citadel Hill, reaching Pyke's back stoop around four o'clock. Mr. and Mrs. Pyke enjoyed Martha's company, and treated her to tea and a plate of hot muffins.

It was almost six o'clock—after nightfall—when Martha continued on to Mrs. Brow's house for the pint tin of molasses. Mrs. Brow's servant said it took Martha only a few minutes to draw the molasses. She was on her way home by six thirty.

Marguery Baird told authorities that come nightfall, she started watching for Martha at the front door. By seven o'clock, she was downright worried. She went to the north barracks to tell her husband, Jacob Baird—a soldier in the Fifty-seventh Regiment—that Martha had not returned home.

Jacob Baird asked permission from Sergeant David Crawford to leave the barracks and search for his stepdaughter. After nearly an hour of searching, he found one of Martha's buckle shoes.

Baird returned to barracks to get help in his search. Richard Chilcott joined him, and together they found Martha's other shoe, and the pint tin of spilt molasses.

It was not until sunrise that Edward Davis and Richard McGuiness, on their way to work, found the girl's naked body at the west corner of the stockade, about two hundred yards from the turnstile. She was partially covered with snow. A doctor later determined that Martha Clough had been raped, and strangled with a strip of cloth torn from her frock.

The authorities arrested Jacob Baird on the evidence of Jonah Smith, who alleged that he had seen Baird and William Hancock with the girl behind Citadel Hill between five o'clock and six o'clock. Smith swore that he had spoken to the two soldiers as he passed them by.

Baird spent nearly a month in jail waiting for trial. Despite the conflicting evidence, no one investigated the murder any further during that time.

At his trial on February 20, the defence council easily proved that Jacob Baird and William Hancock had been in barracks for the entire afternoon and early evening on January 23. When Mr. and Mrs. Pyke swore that Martha had been with them until six o'clock that evening, and Mrs. Brow's servant confirmed that the girl had still been alive at six thirty, Jonah Smith revised his testimony to say he was no longer certain the soldiers he saw with Martha Clough were Baird and Hancock.

The jury required only a few minutes for its foreman, James Deckman, to announce the verdict: not guilty.

If ever a crime had revealed the need for a trained police force in Halifax, this was it. Local magistrates, unaccustomed to criminal investigations, had hastily charged the child's stepfather with the crime. His arrest, detention, and trial took more than a month to conclude. While Jacob Baird sat in jail and stood accused in court, Martha Clough's murderer ran free.

No sooner had the details of the crime and Baird's acquittal been made public than prominent merchants petitioned the Halifax grand jury and the Nova Scotia government for a trained, competent police force. The government responded the way a government well-entrenched in power would, saying "things are well enough as they are." And the grand jury refused the petition on the grounds that "if it raises taxes we are not for it."

ALSO BY BOB KROLL:

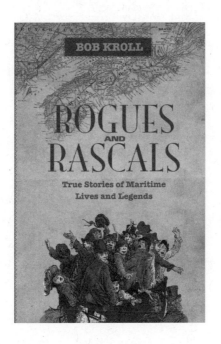